Words I Love to Recite

Words I Love to Recite

An Earthly/Heavenly Dialogue

CHARLES SANTIAGO

RESOURCE *Publications* · Eugene, Oregon

WORDS I LOVE TO RECITE
An Earthly/Heavenly Dialogue

Copyright © 2024 Charles Santiago. All rights reserved. Except for brief quotations in critical publications or reviews, no part of this book may be reproduced in any manner without prior written permission from the publisher. Write: Permissions, Wipf and Stock Publishers, 199 W. 8th Ave., Suite 3, Eugene, OR 97401.

Resource Publications
An Imprint of Wipf and Stock Publishers
199 W. 8th Ave., Suite 3
Eugene, OR 97401

www.wipfandstock.com

PAPERBACK ISBN: 979-8-3852-0721-3
HARDCOVER ISBN: 979-8-3852-0722-0
EBOOK ISBN: 979-8-3852-0723-7

VERSION NUMBER 030124

Though my wife and I have co-authored these poems,
I, for my part, dedicate this book to her,
Elaine Gordon Santiago.

Contents

Introduction | xvii

1. I Avow | 1
2. Hearken to the Angels | 2
3. Bumble | 3
4. Replacing Doubt with Faith in You | 5
5. How I Love This Life! | 6
6. Life Together | 7
7. For Heaven's Sake | 8
8. Doubt | 9
9. Henrietta Swan Leavitt | 10
10. Don't Wait | 11
11. Recite These Rhymes | 12
12. A Palace of Light | 13
13. My ABCs | 14
14. Now I See | 15
15. Dear, Let's Reminisce | 16
16. We Are Joined | 18
17. We Have Found a Way | 19
18. One Life | 20
19. "Welcome, Pilgrim. Welcome, Friend." | 21
20. I Am Learning | 22
21. I Found You, and You Found Me | 23

22. We've a Lovely Passe-Partout | 24

23. Heavenly Gin | 25

24. Time Stands Still | 26

25. I'm Alive! | 27

26. Earthly Bodies | 28

27. A Helping Hand | 29

28. Sweet Communion | 30

29. We're Not Through with Earthly Flings | 31

30. Death Has Made Me See | 32

31. Bodies Past Their Prime on Earth | 33

32. Oh, How Glad I Am! | 34

33. Eyes to See | 35

34. Beyond the Realm of Day and Hour | 36

35. Spirits *Here* and Spirits *There* | 37

36. This Fling of Ours | 38

37. Heaven's Blissful Sea | 39

38. All My Life | 40

39. This Rendezvous | 41

40. Our Heavenly Home | 42

41. Our Love Is Like a Rose | 43

42. Never Think I Left You, Dear | 44

43. The Ladybug | 45

44. Love Is Stronger Than the Grave | 46

45. "It" | 47

46. Laugh with Me | 48

47. We Have Things to Do | 49

48. Nothing More Sacred | 50

49. Much More Than I Knew | 51

50. Goodbye, My Flesh | 52

51. I Resolve | 53

52. I'm All Ears | 54

53. The One Who's Left | 55

54. Spouting Rhymes | 56

55. Blessing and Glory | 57

56. Still Wed | 58

57. This Lovely Fight | 59

58. Every Day and Every Hour | 60

59. Our One, True Life | 61

60. As We Journey, You and I | 62

61. My Closest Kin | 63

62. Relax, My Dear | 64

63. Recite These Words | 65

64. How I Love These Rhymes We Write | 66

65. Doors in Heaven | 67

66. You Are the One | 68

67. You Were There Beholding Me | 69

68. Love Will Be Our Guide | 70

69. Recite Your Creed from Time to Time | 71

70. Words of Cheer | 72

71. True Love | 73

72. Oh, Happy Day! | 74

73. Don't Be Blind | 75

74. Guard This Treasure That We Own | 76

75. Put Your Arms around Me, Dear | 77

76. Love and Praise | 78

77. Higher Ways | 79

78. A Nighttime Blessing | 80

79. Mind to Mind | 81

80. Forty-Two Months | 82

81. Two Homes | 83

82. Good and Kind | 84

83. Here's to *You* | 85

84. This Very Day | 86

85. A Happy Klatch | 87

86. A Life of Union | 88

87. Boldly Clasp My Hand, Above | 89

88. Oh, How Sweet to Be in Love! | 90

89. *Believe*, My Dear | 91

90. A Special Grace | 92

91. Our Wedding Vows | 93

92. Faith in God | 94

93. Here, in Sweet Eternity | 95

94. Earthly Eyes | 96

95. Our Lovely Creed | 97

96. Sailing | 98

97. Earthly Fun | 99

98. Earthly Lies | 100

99. I Will Give This Corpse a Run | 101

100. Intertwined | 102

101. Just a Seed | 103

102. Faith and Love | 104

103. Without a Breath | 105

104. Peace beyond This Earth | 106

105. You're My Adam | 107

106. Rendezvous! | 108

107. Gardens of Delight | 109

108. Daily Bread | 110

109. Our Earthly/Heavenly Tie | 111
110. Death Has Taught Us | 112
111. I'll Remember | 113
112. *Our* Valentine's Day—February 13th | 114
113. My Valentine's Response | 115
114. Yours and Mine | 116
115. Together | 117
116. There Was Never Need to Cry | 118
117. Let's Proceed | 120
118. A Creed | 121
119. Heavenly Kisses | 122
120. A Heavenly Couple | 123
121. Still a Couple | 124
122. *Here* and *There* | 125
123. You Walk with Me | 126
124. The World to Come | 127
125. Quit Your Worrying | 128
126. Spirits Clothed in Clay | 129
127. Watching Movies | 130
128. Content | 131
129. Glimmers | 132
130. Wedding Number Three | 133
131. To Die Is Gain | 134
132. Whisper in My Ear | 135
133. Heaven-Bound | 136
134. Swept Away | 137
135. Heavenly Clothes | 138
136. Wear a Smile | 139
137. A Father's Love | 140

138. Our Present Communion | 141

139. Rejoice and Sing | 142

140. Closer, *Closer* | 143

141. Forty-Three Months | 144

142. Lovers for Eternity | 145

143. Wedding Number Two | 146

144. There's No Reason to Be Sad | 147

145. Because We Are a Unity | 148

146. Our Home, Above | 149

147. Our Home, Above | 150

148. I'll Remember | 151

149. Folks of Old | 152

150. Our Bond Is a River | 153

151. I Concentrate on You | 154

152. Believe in Me | 155

153. Wherever We May Be | 156

154. Now's the Time | 157

155. Believe Me | 158

156. I Can Feel Your Glory | 159

157. Paradise | 160

158. That Silly Fear | 161

159. Now and Here | 162

160. This Love That Cannot Die | 163

161. Speechless | 164

162. Resurrection Bliss | 165

163. Two Homes | 166

164. Meant to Be | 167

165. A Perfect Day | 169

166. In and Out of Time and Space | 170

167. Earthly Trips | 171
168. Clasp My Hand | 172
169. Another Day | 174
170. Three Weddings | 175
171. Fiona's Tune in "Brigadoon" | 176
172. Weddings, Three | 177
173. I Have Learned | 178
174. Heavenly Friends | 179
175. Our Love Survived | 180
176. The Gown I'll Wear | 181
177. Always, *One* | 182
178. A Heavenly Gift | 183
179. It's *You*, Dear | 184
180. You Are Learning *Well* | 185
181. "Heavenly Bride" | 186
182. Trust in God | 187
183. Since Our Second Wedding | 188
184. Remember This | 189
185. *Then*—and *Now* | 190
186. Faith and Love | 191
187. What a Wonder! | 192
188. A Land, Sublime | 193
189. Forbid Me | 194
190. O Light, Divine | 195
191. My Love, My Life | 196
192. Forever, True | 197
193. Death Has Not the Power | 198
194. Yes, You *Are* a Bumblebee | 199
195. The Role of Earthly Beau | 200

196. Whatever Happens | 201

197. I'm Not Dead | 202

198. Life, Above, and Life, Below | 203

199. Not *Really* by Chance | 204

200. Let's Continue | 205

201. Another Earth Month | 206

202. Another Month | 207

203. Tomorrow, Today, and Yesterday | 208

204. The Sweetest Thing | 209

205. Every Day, Our Love Proves True | 210

206. Brand-New Eyes | 211

207. *One* with You, Above | 212

208. The Beauty of the Universe | 213

209. Happiness, Sublime | 214

210. When You Fly | 215

211. I, in You, and You, in Me | 216

212. Suffused with Heaven's Glow | 217

213. Heavenly Creatures | 218

214. Undying Love | 219

215. Deeper in Love | 220

216. Side by Side | 221

217. A Vanquished Foe | 222

218. Read Our Rhymes | 223

219. Why Believe That We Are Through? | 224

220. Hand in Hand, We'll Fly | 225

221. Heaven and Earth | 226

222. Our Home | 227

223. I Believe, Dear | 228

224. With Thee, Dear, *One* | 229

225. Life Awaits | 230

226. Our Holy Union | 231

227. Our Life and Union | 232

228. Our Earthly Love | 233

229. As Time Goes By | 234

230. More Than Memories | 235

231. I Love to Slay This Foe | 236

232. Close Your Eyes and Think of Me | 237

233. Count the Days | 238

234. Dear, Won't It Be Nice! | 239

235. I Think of You and Close My Eyes | 240

236. The Bells of Wedding Number Two | 241

237. I'm So Glad We've Found Our Way! | 242

238. Our Union | 243

239. Our Union, Dear | 244

240. Bodies | 245

241. Just As If | 246

242. Even If Your Body Dies | 247

243. Our Union Will Not Disappear | 248

244. We Are Blessed | 249

245. Providence | 250

246. Mighty Sol | 251

247. In the Stillness of Our Home | 252

248. Think of Me | 253

249. Remind Yourself | 254

250. Stronger Than the Grave | 255

251. Our Heartfelt Plea | 256

252. Beyond My Clay | 257

253. Clasping Hands | 258

254. Trust and Pray | 259

255. A Mighty King | 260

256. Remember Joys We Had Before | 261

257. As I Trek through Timbuktu | 262

258. Doubt's a Monster | 263

259. Our Union Didn't Disappear | 264

260. You, in Me | 265

261. The Beauty of the Earth | 266

262. Close Your Eyes | 267

263. All Your Days on Earth | 268

264. Being Bold | 269

265. A Taste of Heaven | 270

266. Reminding You Is Not a Chore | 271

267. Let's Go On | 272

268. Hard at Work | 273

269. My Happy Solitude | 274

270. Come What May | 275

271. This Heavenly Way | 276

272. My Invited Guest | 277

273. Here and There, High and Low | 278

274. "Clasp Hands, Anew" | 279

275. I Am Very Grateful | 280

276. Our Victory | 281

277. As You Count the Earthly Days | 282

278. What a Silly Thought! | 283

279. Married, Darling, Still, Are We | 284

280. This Life We Share | 285

Introduction

2/24/20 West Palm Beach, Florida. Good morning, my darling. You know how I *love* a trip. With its ups and downs, *still*, dear, I am thrilled to be here with you. Darling, when *you* are happy, *I* am happy. You know it has, *ever*, been so, since we met. The spiritual nature of our bond guarantees our happiness and contentment *wherever* you may find yourself on the world, as it turns. In the long run, money is such a small matter. Worry about it, dear, but not overly much. Sweetheart, we have a vital connection, between us, through the mortal veil that "separates" us. It is a miracle of God, and I am eternally grateful for it. If you think *your* life has changed so completely, just imagine *me*, dear. But, as you wrote on the anniversary card that you gave me in the hospital, the important thing is that we have each other, dear. Yes, sweetheart, that *is* the important thing. I love you so much. Walk your path, dear, where you are, and do not think that you walk it alone. As you go about, on this second day of our mini-vacation, be aware that I am looking through your eyes at the whole experience, and am feeling it, as well, through your walking corpse! :)

So reads my journal entry on a trip to West Palm Beach, Florida from Tallahassee, Florida, on February 24, 2020, seven months after my wife died. At a group counseling session that I attended, it was suggested that we keep a journal of our experience since losing our loved ones. The journal that I started keeping soon turned into a dialogue between me and my wife—a dialogue that confirmed my growing suspicion that I had not *lost* my loved one.

When I finished the journal entry, I *did* take note that my wife referred to me as a walking corpse. I noted it with amusement. I thought of it as a heavenly joke, reminding me of my mortality. I returned to my hotel room—I had been writing in my journal at a picnic table, outside—and got a towel, to lie out in the sun. The warmth from the sun was *so* soothing. I turned on to my stomach, closed my eyes, and luxuriated in the otherworldly pleasure provided by the Florida sun. It wasn't long before I heard the blaring sound of a fire engine as it pulled into the parking lot, right next to me. I started muttering to myself about the great misfortune of not being able to escape the jarring noises of modern day life.

"Sir, sir, are you all right?" I heard the question but it took me a while to realize that the question was being addressed to me. The emergency response person told me that people had seen me lying out in the sun, and reported me to the authorities as a *corpse*—they thought I was dead.

The experience of being referred to, in my journal, as a walking corpse, and the experience of being investigated by emergency personnel as a possible corpse, were separated by a mere ten or fifteen minutes. I had never been referred to as a walking corpse. I had never been the target of attention of emergency personnel on a fire engine, with blaring sirens, checking to see if I was dead—a corpse. I'm pretty certain that a fire engine experience like that will never happen to me again. The juxtaposition of these two bizarre experiences was too much for me to accept as merely a coincidence.

In the four years since my wife died, "coincidences" like the fire engine experience continue to occur. Beyond the experiences, though, is the awareness that our bond of love has not been severed. I (we) have written over 1,700 poems that, often, say much the same thing. The poems never lose their fascination for me, though, because, within their lines, I feel the energy of a continued life. In thirty years of marriage, my wife would, occasionally, bring to my attention that we were soul mates. My wife knew, better than I, the depth of our relationship—not that I would deny we were soul mates—I just didn't have it within me to confront or conceive of life without her around.

After my wife died, I read many books about death and surviving death on a spiritual plane. I took a particular interest in the revival of spiritualism in the late nineteenth century in the United States. In the literature of that revival, I read account after account of supposed communications from the "other side." People wrote of seeing pianos floating up by the ceiling; of seeing men, seated in chairs, being lifted up from the floor miraculously; of hearing musical instruments being played with no visible performers. I concluded that much, if not all, of those types of experiences were due to fanciful imaginations, delusion, or fraud. I believe that communication between the living and the "dead" can and *does* take place, but I think that, the more physical such communication appears to be, the less true it is likely to be. I believe that spiritual communication should be—well, *spiritual*.

Introduction

I have come away from my reading, and from my experience since my wife died, with an unshakable belief in spiritualism, which I suggest is a communication and a communion between the living and the "dead." My fascination with the topic, though, stems from having found communication and communion with the one who called me her soul mate. I believe that the many poems I (we) have written are a reflection of a continued union between a man and a woman who have *not* been separated by death. I believe this is only possible by the power of the Creator of all that is. I believe in God. I, also, believe in my wife.

1. I Avow

Charles Santiago, 12/14/22

I will gladly, now, proclaim
The glory of God's holy name.
Creator of the universe,
I will, now, my verse, rehearse:

> Thou didst make the Earth and Man.
> Thou art Ruler over Pan.
> Woods and fields hold sheep and goats
> Man converts to meat and coats.
> Pan can give to men on Earth,
> Merely, gifts of Earthly worth.

> Thou didst make the sun and Mars—
> Beyond them, all the countless stars.
> Thou art Ruler over Sol.
> In all, Sol plays a minor role.
> Sol's great gifts of warmth and light
> Avail *not*, in the soul's dark night.

Creator of the universe,
Wisdom bids me to be terse.
As in my other rhymes I've said:
"God, indeed, can raise the dead,"
So, in this new book of verse,
I avow I'll need no hearse.

2. Hearken to the Angels, 12/14/22

Highway 27 rest stop north of Perry, Florida

Every day, along my way,
I'm learning, dear, you're here to stay.
"*Alive and here,*" I chant, each day.
"*Dead and gone,*" mere Earthlings say.
I can feel your heav'nly sway,
Keeping doubts and fears at bay.
While I walk, still, bound in clay,
I am, still, the "Devil's" prey.
Angels, in their bright array,
Help me not to go astray.
God, Himself, helps me to pray
"We're a pair, dear, come what may."

Come what may, my Earthly beau,
There's no need to fear "the Foe."
"Dead and gone" he likes to crow.
By now, you've learned that's just NOT SO.
Darling, though you walk, below,
We can bask in heaven's glow.
Goodness! Dear, you, SURELY, know
We've been freed from Earthly woe.
Catch my drift and don't be slow.
Clasp my hand and, dear, let's grow!
Hearken to the angels—oh!
Live where heav'nly breezes blow.

3. Bumble, 12/15/22

In the night is when we shine.
In the night, dear, you are mine.
Wake from sleep and find me, dear,
Just as if you're way up here.
In this garden, we can meet,
While you're resting, off your feet.
Spirits fly, at night, so well.
Close your eyes and you can tell.
Do not fear, my bumblebee.
Bumble, now, and be with me.
Nighttime is the time to see
Splendors of our unity.
Let the Earth spin on its way,
While we savor heaven's day.

Here, in heaven, we can be,
From your doubts, completely, free.
We were joined to be AS ONE,
Even here, beyond the sun.
How I love to meet with you,
Here, above your Timbuktu.
Again, my dear, let's say "I do!"
And feel, inside, how God is true.
More than you can know, my love,
We're alive, up here, above.
Do not let that life, below,
Be the only one you know.
Keep believing, bumblebee,
You're alive, up here, with me.

Remember, dear, that day I died,
And, in our union, you'll abide.
I am here, just like back then,
When I arose to live again.
We are sharing, now, this life,
For, you can tell, I'm, still, your wife.
That day my body died, my dear,
Sealed our union, way up here.
Be patient, darling, there, below.
I'm not gone, as WELL you know.
We will grow in mortal time,
As we share this life, sublime.
Then, my darling, we will be
Free from clay, eternally.

4. Replacing Doubt with Faith in You

Charles Santiago, 12/16/22

Replacing doubt with faith in you
Is just the thing I need to do.
I believe that we can be
Walking, together, in ecstasy.
Faith in you is like a key
That opens the door to eternity.
God meant us to live a life,
Eternally, as man and wife.

Darling, I have learned so much,
Revealing, to me, your heav'nly touch.
How I love that we can be
An Earthly/heavenly unity.
Faith in you is like a sun,
Empow'ring us to shine *as one*.
Holy eyes, God gave to me,
To see our newfound victory.

We have conquered my lying eyes,
Spewing forth their wicked lies.
Oh! my love, we ripped "the veil,"
With God's dear love that cannot fail.
Faith in you is like a dove,
Gently, cooing of God's great love.
Replacing doubt with faith in you,
I'll do, until my days are through.

5. How I Love This Life!

Charles Santiago, 12/17/22

Sacred is our union, dear.
It can never disappear.
Sometimes, it seems that I'm alone,
But, dear, I know, by thee, I'm known.
More than, merely, reminisce,
We can share a heav'nly kiss.
I'm content to live my days,
Seeking you in all my ways.
Finding you, each day, down here,
Makes my Earthly life so dear.
Nothing gives me such delight
As sharing in your heav'nly light.
We can, still, walk, hand in hand,
While I fight Earth's sinking sand.
Sweetheart, how I love this life—
A bumblebee and his dear wife.

6. Life Together, 12/17/22

Aucilla Wildlife Management Area
Gamble Road, near Wacissa, Florida

Sweetheart, I have heard your voice:
"Life, together, is our choice.
We can, still, decide to be
A couple, darling, you and me."

Since the day you "left" my side,
It was simple to decide
I would love you, as my bride,
Till the day I, finally, died.

Sacred, darling, is our love.
I can feel you, from above.
I don't need your body, dear,
To feel you with me, still, down here.

This gift that God has given us,
I'll call our "Resurrection Bus."
I feel freed from time and space,
When we speak, dear, face-to-face.

Darling, when you meet with me,
I'm as happy as can be.
God has been so good to us
To give us tickets for this bus.

Life together, bumblebee—
A gift from God to you and me—
Began that day we said, "I do,"
And never will, my dear, be through.

7. For Heaven's Sake

Charles Santiago, 12/18/22

I'm leaving this world. I cannot stay.
I'm leaving this world for heaven's bright day.
My body is dying, yes, I can see.
Its death won't be, though, the end of me.
I've said it before, and *this* I know:
"I am *not* this body—no!"
God made me to live again,
When I'm done, as Earthly man.

As the sun shines bright, each day,
At night, old Sol has *this* to say:
"Children, God, your Father, shines—
As my mighty light declines—
Shines for you to find the way
To where you're robed, *no more*, in clay.
Learn to see, with heav'nly eyes,
The land where Man, no longer, dies."

Sun and moon and stars, above,
Speak to me of God's great love.
How could God, these wonders make,
Were it not for *heaven's* sake?
I am bound to live, anew,
Once this Earthly life is through.
How could God, my soul, *so* woo,
Unless, *eternal life* were true?

8. Doubt, 12/19/22

Death is not the end of life.
I'm still here. I'm, still, your wife.
Dear, I know you've felt me, THERE,
As we, heav'nly life, now, share.
Believe in God. Believe in me.
It's God who grants us unity.

Conquer doubt, my bumblebee,
If you prize our liberty.
Doubt will close this door we've found
That lets you know I'm still around.
DOUBT, not death, is, now, our foe.
Doubt will fill you full of woe.

I can't touch your skin, my dear,
You must visit me, up here.
Believe WE CAN, my Earthly beau—
We can, heav'nly union, know.
We have come a long, long way,
Since that deathly, fateful day.

"Remember, dear, that day I died,
And, in our union, you'll abide."
While you reach for heaven, love,
I reach down from here, above.
God will help us on our way,
Till you're done with night and day.

9. Henrietta Swan Leavitt, 12/19/22

Greenwise Market, Tallahassee, Florida

Remember THIS, my bumblebee—
You're a, very, part of me!
I'm a, very, part of you,
Though you're still in Timbuktu.
You must get this through your head—
My BODY died, but I'M NOT DEAD!
I am living in your soul.
We will always be one whole.

PATIENT, dear, I'll, always, be
With YOU, my darling bumblebee.
But, oh! the pleasures that we lose,
When you imbibe that Earthly booze.
"Dead and Gone," dear—don't believe it!
I'm HERE, with Henrietta Leavitt.
She and I, now, say to you:
"Be a star that shines, true blue.
Shine with faith in heav'nly union.
Live with us in sweet communion."

10. Don't Wait, 12/20/22

Dear, DON'T WAIT to celebrate.
You can enter heaven's gate.
All is, now, prepared
For US—because you dared
To close your eyes to life on Earth
And join, with me, in heav'nly mirth.
We have found our place,
Beyond the bounds of space.

Joy and peace to all, on Earth,
Who seek, from God, a heav'nly birth.
Life, on Earth, can be
A tryst with heav'nly glee.
Recite these words, on Earth, my love:
"Men, on Earth, can join, ABOVE,
With those who left their clay,
To live in heaven's day."

Join, with me, each day and night,
To celebrate this heav'nly light.
Darling, we are free,
A heav'nly pair, to be!
You don't have to wait to die
To meet, with me, beyond Earth's sky.
We share love, sublime,
Beyond the bounds of time.

11. Recite These Rhymes, 12/20/22

Our thirty Earthly years were FINE.
They joined us in a love, divine.
There's no need to fear
Our love will disappear.
The love we had, back then, has grown,
As angels, dear, to us, have shown,
Into a heav'nly light,
Dispelling Earthly night.

Our heav'nly years, my dear, now, two,
Have been a lovely rendezvous.
God has made us glad,
Through what we thought was sad.
Darling, trust in God and me,
And, all your life, on Earth, will be,
With me, a lovely dance,
As if, in Paris, France.

Recite these rhymes, my bumblebee,
And, quickly, you will learn to see,
Death can, truly, be
A heav'nly victory.
Now, we wait, with bated breath,
Till you, yourself, have conquered death.
Then, we'll rendezvous,
STILL, dear, ME AND YOU.

12. A Palace of Light

Charles Santiago, 12/20/22

Heaven is here—in my house!
It snuck in, as quiet as a mouse.
My house is a palace of light.
It shines, now, through, both, day and night.
Without even dying, I found,
To Earth, I, no longer, am bound.
I breathe, now, a strange, heav'nly breath.
My house is a refuge from death.

Each day, I am coming to see
That angels are visiting me.
I'm thrilled when they knock on my door—
Kind strangers from heaven's bright shore.
Their teachings, I love to espouse,
While meeting, right here, in this house:
"Heaven is right by your side,
If, only, *in love*, you'll abide."

13. My ABCs

Charles Santiago, 12/21/22

I'll, now, recite my ABCs—
A pastime dear to bumblebees.

First, is "A," which stands for "ache"—
"Ache," as in—true hearts that break.
There's no ache that *can* compare
To thinking love's, no longer, there.

Then, comes "B," which stands for "blind"—
"Blind," as in—a narrow mind.
A narrow mind's a thieving cad.
It steals your peace and claims you're mad.

"C," of course, means "freezing cold"—
"Cold," as in—a grief, untold.
One could never *colder*, be
Than thinking *ever* only—*me*.

Struggling, now, is "D," for "death."
Death, one learns, can lose his breath.
I have found that death can be
A doorway to pure ecstasy.

After a while, "L" rolls along—
"L," who sings a dear love song:
"Love's pure light can slay the night
And grant, to blind men, heav'nly sight."

"Z," at last, proclaims her zeal—
Zeal, as shown in love that's real.
Zeal can be a precious friend,
Displaying love that cannot end.

14. Now I See

Charles Santiago, 12/21/22

Now I see I'm born for *this*—
To leave this world, for heaven's bliss.
Mortal, is my body—though—
When it dies, true life, I'll know.
I can feel it in my bones—
Heav'nly love, my spirit, owns.
When my weary bones collapse—
When the bugler rings out "Taps"—
God will claim me, once, for all,
Through a resurrection ball.
I will rise, to live, again,
Beyond the pale of mortal man.
God made Man, indeed, for *this*—
To live, above, in heaven's bliss.

15. Dear, Let's Reminisce, 12/22/22

The day after winter solstice

Dear, let's reminisce, today,
Of days when I was robed in clay.
You and I shared EARTHLY bliss.
We never dreamed of life like THIS.
Lovely, were those days we shared,
When, to be, AS ONE, we dared.
You became my Earthly beau,
As we pledged, true love, to know.
We were living, day and night,
Under Sol's resplendent might.
Those were days of Earthly fun,
Powered by the mighty sun.

Reminisce, with me, my dear,
All those days of Earthly cheer.
How I loved to hold your hand,
Though we dwelt on sinking sand.
How I loved to kiss your lips,
With your hands upon my hips.
How I loved to live with you,
In that Earthly rendezvous!
Life was so much fun,
Beneath the mighty sun.
Darling, you were ALL MY LIFE,
When I became your loving wife.

Now, we live, again, my love,
While I dwell in heaven, "above."
We have learned so much, my dear,
Since you came, with me, "up here."
Life, AGAIN, is so much fun,
As we bask in HEAVEN'S sun.
Dear, I dwell IN YOU,
Till your days are through.
ONE, we ARE, my Earthly beau.
HEAV'NLY love, we've come to know.
We never dreamed of life like THIS—
Joined, AS ONE, in HEAV'NLY bliss!

16. We Are Joined

Charles Santiago, 12/23/22

Yes, my darling, I can feel
How our union, still, is real.
I can sense that you're, still, here.
It's like, your presence, I can *hear*.
These words keep ringing in my head:
Resurrection from the dead.
We are joined, beyond the grave,
Nevermore, to death, a slave.

"Hand in hand," and "side by side"—
These words describe this lovely ride
That God has given, dear, to us,
On heaven's resurrection bus.
Till my days on Earth are through,
I will ride this bus with you.
You and I are blessed to be
In love, for all eternity.

17. We Have Found a Way

Charles Santiago, 12/23/22

I'm content, my pretty bride,
To travel on this pretty ride.
Pretty soon, this ride will end
And, higher, *higher*, we'll ascend.
I recall that day you died,
And, in our union, thus, abide.
We are closer—much more, today,
Though I still reside in clay.
We have found a way to be,
Still, a couple, you and me.

Gone are days of food and drink.
Now, we share a *heav'nly* link.
Yet, somehow, my lovely bride,
In my body, you reside.
In my body, mind, and soul,
We are, still, somehow, one whole.
Heaven walks with me, each day,
Since we found this lovely way.
Let's continue, hand in hand,
Walking in this lovely land.

18. One Life, 12/24/22

I can hear you telling me:
Trust me, sweetheart—you will see—
You and I, still, share one life.
You're, still, my beau. I'm, still, your wife.
Sweetheart, when you mourn and cry,
You proclaim we've said goodbye!
Patiently, my dear, I wait,
Till you open heaven's gate.
After all our lovely rhymes,
You hark back to grieving times!
Resurrection from the dead—
Sweetheart, get that through your head.
IT'S TRUE! I'm walking next to you,
THERE, my dear, in Timbuktu.
If you think I'm gone, my dear,
WHAT ON EARTH will make you hear?
Trust your hunches, bumblebee—
Live in heaven, HERE, with me.

19. "Welcome, Pilgrim. Welcome, Friend."

Charles Santiago, 12/25/22, inspired by a Christmas Eve service at Trinity United Methodist Church, Tallahassee, Florida

When we're done with life on Earth,
We'll ascend to heav'nly mirth.
Untold multitudes await
To welcome us through heaven's gate.
Oh! what joy and heav'nly bliss—
To meet and share with them a kiss.

> "Welcome, pilgrim. Welcome, friend.
> Enjoy this bliss that has no end.
> Oh, what joy to meet with you,
> Now that you, with flesh, are through!
> Come inside and feel at peace,
> *Here*, where Earthly troubles cease.
> We rejoice with you, today,
> Now that you are here to stay.
> You will meet a mighty throng
> Who've been with you, friend, all along.
> They will help you to grow strong,
> *Here*, our friend, where you belong.
> Do not fret and do not fear.
> We're so glad that you are here."

In our happy home, above,
We'll be with the ones we love.
Gone will be all pain and woes,
When we don our heav'nly clothes.

20. I Am Learning

Charles Santiago, 12/25/22

You've preceded me, my love,
To our home in heaven, "above."
Still, it's joy to share, with you,
Life, down here, in Timbuktu.

I am learning, by and by,
Not to mourn and not to cry.
What a dunce, my dear, am I,
To think our love could ever die.

I remember what you said—
The words keep ringing in my head:
"Do you think I'd leave you, dear,
Just because I've come *up here?*"

I refuse to be death's pawn.
"Dead and Gone" is dead and gone.
We are *spirits*, joined, *as one*.
Heaven, for us, has, now, begun.

Well I know these truths are *so*.
I rehearse them here, below.
Sweetheart, I'm your heav'nly beau,
While, on Earth, I, still, must grow.

21. I Found You, and You Found Me, 12/26/22

Dear, our union thrills me *so*,
As we *ever* onward, go.
One, in heaven, and *one*, on Earth,
I have never known such mirth.

Before we even met, my dear,
Angels built our home, up here.
I found you, and you found me
And, thus, we found eternity.
Can't you feel how life, below,
Is filled with heaven's lovely glow?

Intertwined with you, above,
How I feel God's wondrous love!
Life, for me, on Earth, below,
Indeed, is filled with heaven's glow!

Darling, you're a joy to me,
As we sail on heaven's sea.
God is guiding me and you
On such a lovely rendezvous.
My beloved Earthly beau,
Can you feel our love, still, grow?

Resurrection bells, my dear,
Ring for me, each day, down here.
I can feel your heav'nly glow,
While I struggle here, below.

Grow your faith, my bumblebee,
Every day, with heav'nly glee.
Faith and work and love, my dear,
Spread, for us, a table, HERE.
Can you feel our heav'nly mirth,
In the beauty of the Earth?

22. We've a Lovely Passe-Partout, 12/27/22

Inspired by a car ride down Highway 27, Florida

Darling, we will, always, rhyme.
We're not bound by space and time.
Though you dwell in Timbuktu,
With its bound'ries, we are through.
We've a lovely passe-partout.
To time and space, we bid, "Adieu."
Side by side, we're on a ride,
Traveling on the "other side."
Our home, my dear, is way up here,
In heaven's lovely atmosphere.
You have died, with me, to be
Free from grim mortality.
Any place, on Earth, you go,
We can, timeless rapture, know.

I have learned it's really true—
This lovely tale I hear from you.
We are freed, my dear, to be
Walking in eternity.
I'm not blind. I've learned to see—
You, still, walk down here with me.
Heaven found us out, my dear,
While my body's, still, down here.
How I love to take a ride
In the car—down on "this side."
Though the tires stay on the ground,
Up, to heaven, dear, we're bound.
Heaven's such a lovely "place,"
Freeing me from time and space.

23. Heavenly Gin, 12/27/22

Another month, my heav'nly bride,
Since that day your body died.
I have learned you know my life,
Like a doting, heav'nly wife.
People think I'm crazy, dear,
To think you're, still, with me, down here.
Crazy's what I want to be,
If I can walk, dear, still, with thee.
Let another month begin—
I'll keep drinking heav'nly gin.

Drink your heav'nly gin, my dear,
If it brings you, CLEAR UP HERE.
"Heav'nly gin," I know, my love,
Is just your faith in God, above.
You are HERE, in heaven, with me,
While I am THERE, my dear, with thee.
Another month of Earthly days—
Our hearts, with love, are all ablaze.
Darling, God will see us through
All your days in Timbuktu.

24. Time Stands Still

Charles Santiago, 12/28/22

Once again, my heav'nly bride,
Speaking from the "other side,"
I can hear you, loud and clear:
"You are with me, dear, *up here.*"
I can feel it's *you*, my love,
Lifting me to heaven, above.
When I feel your joy, like this,
I know we're joined in *heaven's* bliss.
Time stands still, and I can feel
Everlasting life is real.
Death is just a pure charade,
Mocking heaven's great parade.

Since the day your body died,
You've been here, right by my side.
As I learn, dear, not to cry,
I can feel the by-and-by.
God has given you and me
A home in bright eternity.
The past and future disappear,
As, *now*, I feel that you are near.
You, who walked with me on Earth,
Share, with me, your heav'nly mirth.
I know—that day—I died with you,
For, dear, I, now, abide with you.

25. I'm Alive! 12/28/22

I have not forgotten you!
Our life together isn't through.
Keep believing I'm alive,
Beyond an Earthly 9 to 5.
I'm not gone, my bumblebee.
I'm closer, dear, than you can see.
More and more, you'll see, my love,
I didn't leave you for heaven, "above."
Here, in heaven, we love to be
With loved ones who, from Earth, break free.
Heaven, dear, is YOU AND ME,
Still, my love, a He and She.

26. Earthly Bodies, 12/29/22

Do not think it strange, my dear,
That Earthly bodies disappear.
Earthly bodies must obey
The laws that govern Earthly clay.
Was I just my clay, my love?
Don't we have a home, above?

Eve and Adam live, today,
Though they're done with Earthly clay.
God made Man to live, once more,
On a bright eternal shore.
What is strange, my bumblebee,
Is THIS: to think Man couldn't be—
Couldn't be alive, again—
After death, a HEAV'NLY man.

You and I have learned a lot,
Since the day we tied the knot.
Most of all, we've come to know,
Death is not Man's fatal foe.
It, only, SEEMS that death has won,
When people finish out their run.
Man is meant to correspond
With God in an eternal bond.
You and I have learned it's SO,
As we both rejoice and grow.

27. A Helping Hand

Charles Santiago, 12/29/22

This life I live on Earth, my friend,
Will, soon enough, come to an end.
But I am sure that I will live
A brand-new life that God will give.
When time and space are through with me,
I'll soar into eternity.
My soul will never die.
My home's beyond the sky.

My Father is Almighty God.
He's clothed me and, my feet, He's shod.
He guides me through this life, below,
Until it's time for me to go.
He loves me as His child, I know.
He made me, and He bids me grow.
Oh! that I may see,
How, like Him, to be.

If I see you on the road
That leads, above, to my abode,
I will try, to you, to lend,
A helping hand, my Earthly friend.
Selfishness has plagued me *so*,
All my years on Earth, below.
Oh! that I could be,
From selfishness, set free.

28. Sweet Communion, 12/30/22

What a thrill, my bumblebee,
When you see that we can be
Closer than we were, BEFORE—
Before I passed through heaven's door.
Holy angels guide us, dear,
To our mansion, way up here.
PATIENCE, darling—you will see
How to be alive with me.
Since I've passed through heaven's gate,
You and I can celebrate
Sweet communion, face-to-face,
Beyond the bounds of time and space.
God, our Father, gives us, love,
Holy pleasure HERE, above.
Holy union, dear, is ours,
Up, above all Earthly powers.

When you came here, yesterday—
When you left behind your clay—
THEN, began, my darling beau,
Higher joys that we now know.
Believe me, darling, we can be
Joined in heaven's ecstasy.
When you "hugged me in my shroud,"
Angels gathered in a crowd.
"We will help this man," they said,
"Learn to leave, behind, the dead."
ALIVE, my darling, are we, two—
YOU in ME, and I in YOU.
Don't you EVER think, my dear,
I left you when I came up here.
Hand in hand, my bumblebee,
We enjoy eternity.

29. We're Not Through with Earthly Flings, 12/30/22

Darling, we have found our place,
Meeting, NOW, dear, face-to-face.
All the things our rhymes have said—
How we live beyond the dead—
Are true, my darling bumblebee.
We're, STILL, a team, dear, you and me.
I love you SO, my Earthly beau,
As, through eternity, we go.
You believe I'm THERE, with you.
You believe our life's not through.
God gave you a passe-partout.
We can, still, dear, woo and coo.
Let us take another trip.
Heav'nly gin, we, both, will sip.
We're not through with Earthly flings—
Let's take off for Tarpon Springs.
Book our room at Hampton Inn.
Let the new year's joys begin.
Twenty, twenty-three will be
A year for heav'nly ecstasy.

30. Death Has Made Me See

Charles Santiago, 12/30/22

Forty-one months have passed, my dear,
And I, still, feel that you're, still, here.
I have learned to court you, love,
Though you live in heaven, above.
Heaven's *above*, and heaven's *below*—
Heaven's *wherever*, my dear, we go.
More and more, I feel your glow,
As I continue, down here, to grow.
Heaven is such a glorious place—
It's *in* and *out* of time and space.

The thirty years we shared on Earth
Blossom, now, in heav'nly mirth.
One we are, and *one* we'll be,
Now and through eternity.
Goodness! Dear, I'd never guess
What could come from just a "yes."
Yes! I'll woo you, till I die,
And leave behind this Earthly sky.
Eternal love and eternal life—
They're just the thing for man and wife.

"Goodbye," my dear, we never said,
That day that they pronounced you dead.
I was there, at your last breath—
That day you triumphed over death.
I can feel your vict'ry, dear,
Though I linger, still, down here.
God is kind to give to Man
The gift of living, once again.
Darling, death has made me see,
God has claimed us, you and me.

31. Bodies Past Their Prime on Earth, 1/1/23

Our spirits, darling bumblebee,
From the sting of death, are free.
The clay with which we're robed, on Earth,
Is barred from everlasting mirth.
"I am not my body—no!"
This truth, you, often, claim to know.
Speak, dear, as a heav'nly sage:
"Bodies, though destroyed by age,
Release the spark of light, within,
That flies above, to heaven's inn.
In the twinkling of an eye,
Beleaguered souls, to heaven, fly."

When released from time and space,
Spirits find their proper place.
Darling, you have sense to know
There's more to life than what's below.
Bodies, past their prime on Earth,
Revive to everlasting mirth.
Infirmity and pain and gloom
Disappear, beyond the tomb.
Don't be fooled by Earthly eyes—
Life awaits, beyond the skies.
Bodies, ravaged, below, by time,
Ascend to heaven's life, sublime.

32. Oh, How Glad I Am!

Charles Santiago, 1/1/23
Tarpon Springs, Florida

Let me, now, rehearse my creed:
God can raise the dead, indeed!
"Dead and gone," you're *not*, my dear.
You still live with me, down here.
Souls in love, God joined as *one*,
Live beyond the Earth and sun.
I can feel you smile, my love,
All the way from heav'n, above.
Laugh with me. I'll laugh with you,
While we pass through Timbuktu.
We have found we, still, can be
Lovebirds, filled with ecstasy.

Yes! We, still, can have our flings;
So—I've come to Tarpon Springs.
How I love to reminisce
The times we shared here—Earthly bliss!
What a gift, my dear, was ours,
When we shared those Earthly hours!
Oh! How glad I am that we
Can, now, enjoy eternity.
Twenty, twenty-three is here,
And *we* are, still, together, dear.
Our Maker loves us, dear, so much,
He shows us how to stay in touch.

33. Eyes to See, 1/2/23

Tarpon Springs, Florida

Bumble to your heart's content,
In an inn or in your tent.
You will find, my bumblebee,
You will not be far from me.
How I love to be with you,
In all these Earthly things you do!
"Pretend," my darling, I am THERE,
And you will find me everywhere.
In your heart, I DO abide.
From my love, you cannot hide.

Just as you are seeking me,
Darling, I am seeking thee.
Remember what I've said to you:
"There's a lot that I can do."
Death cannot keep us apart.
Like you've said, "We share one heart."
Believe the lovely things you see—
They are not mere fantasy.
I would never leave you, dear,
Though I live in heaven, "up here."

You are right, my Earthly beau—
I am with you where you go.
There's no need, my dear, to wait,
This heav'nly love, to consummate.
Heav'nly joys are HERE, for us,
On this resurrection bus.
I can see, my bumblebee—
You have eyes, dear, just for ME!
It should be quite plain to see—
I have eyes, dear, just for thee.

34. Beyond the Realm of Day and Hour

Charles Santiago, 1/2/23
Tarpon Springs, Florida

There's a heav'nly world *within*—
Within this clay, my heav'nly inn.
I can, with the angels, talk.
I can, with my loved ones, walk.
God, who made the Earth and stars,
Whisks me far beyond our Mars.
I'm a child of heav'nly light,
Fashioned by God's love and might.

I am thrilled to feel the power,
Beyond the realm of day and hour.
God, my Maker, says to me:
"I made you, with Me, to be.
Don't you worry. You will see,
You can grasp eternity.
When your days on Earth are through,
There'll be more for you to do."

Here, below, on planet Earth,
I am filled with heav'nly mirth.
Oh, the joy, to realize
I will live, beyond Earth skies!
This clay that is my heav'nly inn
Is just a lovely, outer skin.
Deep within, I know that I
Have a gift—I will not die.

35. Spirits *Here* and Spirits *There*, 1/2/23

Tarpon Springs, Florida

I will self-induce a trance,
To meet with you, dear, not by chance.
Do your part, as I do mine,
And we will savor love, divine.
As we exercise our wills,
We'll experience heav'nly thrills.
Why should we not meet, above,
Thrilled by our eternal love?
I have been remiss to think,
Our souls, my dear, we couldn't link.
"Dead and Gone," indeed, is strong.
He even makes *me* think *what's wrong*—
I who know you're, still, "*down here*,"
For, I can feel you, still, are near.
Spirits *here* and spirits *there*,
Still, can meet, dear, if they dare.

I am anxious, bumblebee,
For you to come and visit me.
Like we've said: "Two homes, have WE"—
Two homes to share our ecstasy.
Close your eyes and lift your soul.
You will feel how we're, still, whole.
We would be remiss to think
That FLESH was, dear, our only link.
We can, now, perfect our bond,
As, to love, we, both, respond.
We will, dear, our souls, unite,
In heav'nly day and Earthly night.
Why should we not grow our love,
Down, below, and up, above?
While the Earth goes round the sun,
We'll perfect what we've begun.

36. This Fling of Ours, 1/3/23

Tarpon Springs, Florida

Darling, I abide in you,
Just like you abide in me.
My life on Earth is, still, not through,
Though, from a body, I am free.

Souls in heaven, still, abide
In Time and Space, if, SO, they choose.
You, still, feel me, as your bride.
Our union, dear, we will not lose.

Love me, darling, every day.
How God loves, both, you and me!
From His love, we will not stray.
He made us for eternity!

HERE AND NOW, my bumblebee,
I can, still, enjoy with you.
Now and then, you come to see,
JUST how strong is heav'nly glue.

"DEATH, OUR UNION, COULD NOT BREAK"—
Write these words, dear, in your heart.
When doubters try, your faith, to shake,
Recite those words, your heav'nly chart.

This fling of ours, in Tarpon Springs,
Is heaven, dear, my Earthly beau.
We're soarin', as if on eagles' wings.
All done, are we, with Earthly woe.

37. Heaven's Blissful Sea

Charles Santiago, 1/3/23
Indian Rocks Beach, Florida
Inspired by "Passing Baldo's Tower" by Will Ackerman

Perfect peace, my love,
Comes to me from thee, above.
You have found me, seeking you,
And filled me, through and through,
With heaven's deep serenity,
As we sail this blissful sea.

Heaven's blissful sea, my dear,
Reaches all the way down here.
We board our ship and sail away
To some bright, eternal day.
Peace, like this, I've never known.
It's a peace, dear, all our own.

You and I, aboard this ship,
Enjoy a lovely, heav'nly trip.
I can feel eternity,
Calling you, and calling me:
"Love will, always, lead you two,
To the life that's good and true."

38. All My Life, 1/4/23

Tarpon Springs, Florida

Darling, you are ALL MY LIFE.
I am your devoted wife.
DIVINE, my darling, is our bond.
You and I, TO GOD, respond.
We could not, FOREVER, live,
Were it not, for GOD, to give.
MY OTHER SELF are you, my dear,
In this life we live, up here.
How I love you, bumblebee!
God meant you, dear, just for me.

God meant *you* for *me*, my love,
Down, below, or up, above.
My other self are *you*, my dear.
Without you, dear, I'd disappear.
Let's continue, all our life,
One, my darling—man and wife.
Like one and one, my dear, are two,
You are me, and I am you.
All my life are you, to me—
Signed, your loving bumblebee.

39. This Rendezvous, 1/4/23

Tarpon Springs, Florida

Come, my darling, let us fly,
Far beyond the Earthly sky.
Put your Earthly car in gear,
And we will travel, way up here.
While you gaze on Earthly scenes,
We will splice our heav'nly genes—
We will join, AS ONE,
Beyond Earth's mighty sun.

On this trip we're taking, dear,
Mighty angels will appear.
They will take us where you'll see
Glimpses of eternity.
We'll rejoice, AS ONE, above,
Far beyond an Earthly love.
These trips are so much fun,
Uniting us, AS ONE.

Darling, when we take these flings,
THERE, on Earth, to Tarpon Springs,
Time and Space deliver us
Far above that Earthly fuss.
Death became a ticket to
This rendezvous for me and you.
Come with me, my dear,
To pleasures, way up here.

40. Our Heavenly Home

Charles Santiago, 1/4/23
Hampton Inn and Suites lobby
Tarpon Springs, Florida

Darling, I've enjoyed our fling.
I'm feeling like a mighty king.
You have proved to me, once more,
We've a home on heaven's shore.
My body is our home, below,
But, oh, to heaven, I can go!
Our heav'nly home's not *up*, in space.
It's not down *here*, in any place.
Our heav'nly home is, when, by grace,
We commune, dear, face-to-face.
You did not go far away,
When you left your clay that day.
I can feel, sometimes, my dear,
We're closer than when you were here.

Our heav'nly home is hard to see,
But *this* I know, dear—we can be
Living here, on Earth, below,
While we bask in heaven's glow.
"Soul mates," dear, you said we were.
Heavens! Love, I *do* concur.
We are, still, a couple, dear,
Though I'm stuck in clay, down here.
When I drive back to our house,
There, I'll meet with you, my spouse.
"It's good to go," you used to say,
"But **I** am glad we're back today."
It, still, is fun to go for flings,
Especially, here, in Tarpon Springs.

41. Our Love Is Like a Rose, 1/5/23

Tarpon Springs, Florida

We are ONE, my bumblebee,
Though, at times, it's hard to see.
Always, darling, think of me
As living there, on Earth, with thee.
Yes, it's hard to understand
How we dwell in heaven's land,
But we have found it's true—
Our love is never through.

Remember THIS, my Earthly beau—
All your days, our love will grow.
"Forget me not," means "I'm, still, here,
And, to YOU, dear, I'll appear."
I, from you, am not remote.
Death, for us, presents no moat.
We are souls who see
Beyond Earth's deep blue sea.

Sweetheart, you're my Earthly man.
I love to hear you say, "We can!"
Cast away your doubts, my love.
Join me in our home, "above."
We have come a long, long way,
Since that final, Earthly day.
Our love is like a rose—
A rose that, ALWAYS, grows.

42. Never Think I Left You, Dear, 1/5/23

Greenwise Market, Tallahassee, Florida

I KNOW you, dear, and all you do,
Way down there, in Timbuktu.
I LOVE you, dear. I wish you knew,
JUST how CLOSE I am to you.
"*I* found YOU, and YOU found ME
And, thus, we found eternity."
Sweetheart, do not think I'm dead!
Erase that image from your head.
Darling, feel me by your side.
How I love to be your bride!
You can feel me—Yes, I know.
What a joy, with you, to grow!

Always, dear, review our creed:
"Our life on Earth is just a seed.
We will live, forever, dear,
In a land devoid of fear.
You are NOT your body, love.
You live HERE, with me, above.
Death was just an entrance way
To this life we have, today.
We still walk, dear, hand in hand,
In a lovely, heav'nly land."

How I love our Earthly flings,
Way down there, in Tarpon Springs.
We have had some lovely times,
Dreaming up some Tarpon rhymes.
Now, we're back at our home base—
Living, still, dear, face-to-face.
Never think I left you, dear,
When I came to live, "up here."

43. The Ladybug

Charles Santiago, 1/6/23

Darling, what a dunce I'd be,
If I thought you couldn't see
All that, *here*, pertains to me,
In this world of Earth and sea.

In this world of night and day,
Surely, I'd have lost my way,
If I thought you couldn't stay
With your Earth mate, come what may.

The ladybug—the dog—the hawk—
Gave to me, dear, such a shock.
You and I are guided by
God Almighty's searching eye.

God Almighty made us, dear,
So we couldn't disappear.
You and I have eyes to see
More than just the Earth and sea.

Every day, I see how we
Are walking in eternity.
Our union will not disappear,
While I'm trapped in clay, down here.

44. Love Is Stronger Than the Grave, 1/7/23

If you say, "I'm missing her,"
With the dragon, you concur—
The dragon, DEATH, who says that I
Am DEAD AND GONE, beyond Earth's sky.

Don your armor, every day,
And the dragon, you will slay.
Mount your steed and grab your spear.
Make that dragon disappear.

The dragon fights, with all his power,
To make you DOUBT for just an hour.
DOUBT can throw you off your steed.
Death is crafty—yes, indeed.

Remember all the things we've done,
Since I finished out my run.
Are they all, dear, just a dream?
Are things really like they SEEM?

I am NOT, dear, JUST A DREAM!
Things are NOT just what they SEEM.
Love is stronger than the grave.
Death is just a lying knave.

Count your blessings, bumblebee.
You have faith with which to see.
Our union is no fleeting dream.
Things are not, dear, what they SEEM.

45. "It," 1/7/23

Inspired by the film *Adventure* (1945)
Starring Clark Gable and Greer Garson

Live your life, dear. Live your life!
I am with you, all the way.
I'm your everlasting wife—
Not for just an Earthly day.

Clark Gable, dear, you ARE, to ME.
Greer Garson, dear, I AM, to THEE.
Heav'nly knowledge is the tree
That makes us, dear, a He and She.

Live your life, my bumblebee!
Adventure is our destiny.
Like two sailors, on a ship,
Our heav'nly gin, we have, to sip.

We have found what Clark calls "It"—
Grit to fight and never quit.
Heav'nly bliss is ours, to share,
Even NOW—because we DARE.

46. Laugh with Me, 1/7/23

Dear, you've come, again, to say:
"I am with you, dear, today.
How I love to be with you!
How I love our rendezvous!
Dear, it's thrilling just to be
Bumbling with my bumblebee!
Sigh a sigh of great relief—
We are done with tears of grief.
Joy, beyond our wildest dreams,
In our hearts, from heaven, beams.
Darling, God is kind to us,
Lifting us from worldly fuss.
We can, with the angels, talk.
We can, through the heavens, walk.
We, to heav'nly bliss, are wed,
Above the kingdom of the dead.
We are living, free of dread.
We partake of heav'nly bread.
God designed, for you and me,
Life, above Earth's reverie.
Laugh with me, my Earthly beau.
It's a thrill, this joy, to know."

47. We Have Things to Do, 1/10/23

Life, for us, is good and true.
Darling, I'm not leaving you.
You're afraid, with passing time,
We'll forget, dear, how to rhyme.
Time and Space can't box us in.
We've a home, above Earth's din.
Live to be a hundred, dear—
We'll, still, have our home, up here.
Dead and gone, I'll never be.
Our love is for eternity.
Though your body waste away,
I'll be with you, every day.
To live my life, my bumblebee,
I'm not called away from thee.

Put your doubts and fears away.
Our life and love are here, to stay.
God has joined us, bumblebee,
For now, and for eternity.
When the sun has lost its glow,
Sweet communion, we'll, still, know.
We have earned the right to be
An everlasting unity.
Earthly thoughts, dear—let them go.
Be, all done, with Earthly woe.
Claim this house we have, up here.
It's closer than you think, my dear.
We have things to do, my love,
Forever and a day—above.

48. Nothing More Sacred

Charles Santiago, 1/10/23

We, all, have our roads that we walk here, below.
Their ultimate meaning, *in heaven*, we'll know.
Our friends and our neighbors and enemies, too,
Are helping us, always, to learn what is true.
Absurd, it may seem, to the casual eye,
How scoundrels and saints, both, live in this sty.
In heaven, we'll see how the meanest of men
Were guided by God, like a mothering hen,
To learn, in the end, from their murders and lies,
There's nothing more sacred, beneath Earthly skies,
Than love for each other, and heavenly ties.

49. Much More Than I Knew

Charles Santiago, 1/10/23

I *have* you, my darling. I *have* you.
I have you, much more than I knew.
I have you inside of my soul.
Without you, I wouldn't be whole.
I'm strongest, my darling, above,
When filled with our infinite love.

I *have* you, by dint of God's power.
I *have* you for each Earthly hour.
It's *you*, dear, today, as back *then*.
You died, but you're living, again.
Beyond all the things that I do,
Is everything done, dear, *by you*.

My darling, you're living *in me*,
But, *how*, dear, I really can't see.
I'm loving each moment we live
This life that God, *only*, can give.
I *have* you, my darling. I *have* you.
I have you, much more than I knew.

50. Goodbye, My Flesh

Charles Santiago, 1/11/23

Goodbye, my flesh. I need you, no more.
My spirit has flown to heaven's bright shore.
I leave you, below, to rot or to burn.
You've served me well, my lessons, to learn.
I'll remember your form, in this new life, above.
God made you for me, by His power and love.

People will say that I'm gone or asleep.
Without understanding, they'll mourn, and they'll weep.
Your eyes, they will shut. Your arms, they will fold.
"Rest," they will say, "where you'll never grow old.
Gone is this soul who once walked on Earth,
Far, far away, to heavenly mirth."

"Rest" in the grave, or be burned by the fire,
As, "way up to heaven," I, now, will "retire."

In heavenly splendor, I'll, still, walk, below,
Praying, my loved ones will notice my glow.
I hope they won't say that I'm *dead* and I'm *gone*.
I hope they will sense me in heaven's bright dawn.
My loved ones, on Earth, are a heaven, to me.
With faith, hope, and love, we, all, can be free.

51. I Resolve

Charles Santiago, 1/12/23

Darling, when I concentrate—
When I, truly, contemplate—
Heaven's joy descends,
As my soul ascends.

How I'm thrilled to leave this place,
And be so filled with God's dear grace,
That I can feel your hand
Touch my wedding band.

Death has opened up this door
To heaven's brightly gleaming shore.
We're like king and queen,
O'er lands I've never seen.

Let us reign, my heav'nly bride,
Somewhere on that Other Side,
And leave, behind, this mess
Of Earthly gruesomeness.

We're a team—and I declare!
I run my fingers through your hair.
We can hug and kiss,
In heaven's wondrous bliss.

As I muse and contemplate,
I resolve to concentrate
On *you*, my lovely bride,
And, in God's peace, abide.

52. I'm All Ears

Charles Santiago, 1/12/23

Heavens, dear! I *know* you're *here*,
And I can hardly wait,
With *you*, to celebrate.

If we can kiss, *down here*, like this,
What joy we'll have, my love,
When I reach home, *above*!

This Earthly life, my heav'nly wife,
Is like a trip to Mars—
To Venus and the stars.

Keep confiding. *Keep* abiding.
I'm all ears, my dear,
To hear you speak, down here.

53. The One Who's Left, 1/12/23

We are closer, bumblebee,
Now that I, from clay, am free.
*God has taught us, you and **me**,*
*How, eterni**ty**, to **see**.*
In the spirit, we are ONE,
While you finish out your run.

LOVE, my darling, binds us to
GOD, whose love is EVER true.
*Enjoy, with me, our rendez**vous**,*
*Below and **through** the sky, so **blue**.*
In the spirit, you and I
Travel through the Earthly sky.

Souls like ours, dear, joined, AS ONE,
Live beyond the Earth and sun.
*When one's Earthly life is **done**,*
*Heaven's **won**. True life's be**gun**.*
The one who's left, still, on the Earth,
Receives the other's heav'nly mirth.

54. Spouting Rhymes

Charles Santiago, 1/13/23

Yes, my dear, I'm seeking you.
I'll seek you, till my life is through.
"Seek and find," says Holy Writ,
Spurring me to faith and grit.
You are *here* for me to find.
I can feel our souls aligned.
You haven't left me far behind.
I *can see*, dear. I'm not blind.

People think that you're not here.
They don't think you're even near.
Even churchmen say to me,
"She is gone, man. Can't you see?"
"Dead and gone," is all I hear.
I can *feel* how people sneer.
I'm resolved to seek, alone,
Like a dog who hides his bone.

At times, I feel you close to me—
Closer than my *skin* can be.
At times, I wonder, like the rest.
Am I nuts, or am I blessed?
I'd be *crazy*, dear, for you.
("He's here, again, that 'you know who.'")
I'm just spouting rhymes, my dear.
Of course, I know you're, always, here.

55. Blessing and Glory, 1/14/23

GOD is He, my bumblebee,
Who gives this life to you and me.
GOD is She, my Earthly beau,
Who causes you and me to grow.
You and I are ONE, my love,
Because we, two, are "guilty" of
Loving God with all our heart.
Worthy of praise, O God, Thou art.
Blessing and glory we give to Thee,
Creator, Sustainer, of all we see.

56. Still Wed 1/14/23

Darling, since I left my clay,
I've been with you, every day.
Live, down there, and, come what may,
I'll be with you, all the way.

No matter, dear, what others say,
Your love is causing no delay
For me to enter heaven's way.
Let me, now, your fears, allay:

> Spirits, freed from Time and Space,
> Still, can show up, any place.
> Heaven's not a place TO GO.
> Heaven, FREEDOM, is to know.

I am living there, with you,
In all the Earthly things you do.
Sweetheart, wear your wedding band.
We're still wed in heaven's land.

57. This Lovely Fight

Charles Santiago, 1/15/23

Greater than the signs you send,
Is knowing, dear, that we, still, blend.
Really, there's no need to fear,
My dear, that you're, no longer, here.
Flesh and Blood has lost the fight,
Though he roar, with all his might.
I have learned to fear, no more,
The power of his mighty roar.

Friends in heaven and friends on Earth
Join, *as one*, in heav'nly mirth.
Angels lift this veil, below,
And share, with men, their heav'nly glow.
Thank you, dear, for loving me,
And showing how, from death, we're free.
We've put death, himself, to sleep.
Forever, now, he's counting sheep.

I resolve, with all my might,
To fight, my dear, this lovely fight.
Though I've won, I, still, must learn,
Patiently, to wait my turn—
My turn to hear, all heaven, sing—
To me—a victor in the ring.
Hand in hand, we, then, will soar,
And be harassed, by death, no more.

58. Every Day and Every Hour, 1/15/23

Sweetheart, have more faith in me!
Be aware that I can be,
Daily, seeking you, my love,
As you're seeking me, above.

Just like you are seeking me,
Sweetheart, I am seeking thee.
Believe me—I'm, still, loving you,
As you pass through Timbuktu.

In the spirit, dear, we must
Learn, each other, now, to trust.
In the spirit, come what may,
I am with you, day by day.

Be aware that I'M aware
Of the life we have, down there.
Just remember, bumblebee,
God is guiding you and me.

Sweetheart, trust in angels, too.
How they love to help us, two.
"Trust your hunches," I have said.
Angels, all around you, tread.

We are spirits, bumblebee.
Trust in God and trust in me.
Every day and every hour,
We enjoy this heav'nly power.

59. Our One, True Life, 1/15/23

Greenwise Market, Tallahassee, Florida

While all around me, chaos reigns,
I am making heav'nly gains.
Our love is strong and, dear, remains
Alive and well on Earthly plains.
While my Earthly body wanes,
I am sev'ring Earthly chains.
In the midst of Earthly strains,
Heav'nly peace, my soul, attains.
In the midst of floods and rains,
Angels sing such sweet refrains.

Heav'nly voices praise God's name.
Let us join them and proclaim:
"God's dear love remains the same.
To *ever* praise Him is our aim."
God removes our Earthly shame.
Now, our heav'nly home, we claim.
Earthly wealth and power and fame,
I forsake as, all, too tame.
God—our one, *true life*—became.
Our hearts, to Him, are all aflame.

Our hearts, to God, are all aflame.
Let us ever praise His name!
My one, true beau on Earth, below,
Let us ever upwards, go.
Earthly life is, all, too tame.
Let's make heav'nly joy our aim.
Soon, your days will, all, be through.
To Earthly clay, you'll say, "Adieu."
Death and pain will, no more, be
A part of us, my bumblebee.

60. As We Journey, You and I, 1/17/23

Resurrection from the dead
Takes away my Earthly dread.
Darling, I can feel your glow.
We've outfoxed Man's ancient foe.
We are children of the light.
God, our Father, grants us sight.
As we gaze upon God's face,
We resume our rightful place.
Joy from heaven fills my soul.
You and I have reached our goal.

As we journey, you and I,
In the lovely by-and-by,
Time, itself, must bend the knee.
Time can't block our ecstasy.
Gone is, now, mortality.
Death must bow to you and me.
Since God raised you from the dead,
I've been fed with heav'nly bread.
I can taste eternity,
Since you've claimed your bumblebee.

SACRED *is our union, dear.*
It can banish Earthly fear.
You and I have not been fooled—
By the angels, we've been schooled.
We can, still, maintain our ties.
There's no need for sad goodbyes.
Man and wife, we, still, can be,
Now, and for eternity.
Since you've claimed your heav'nly wife,
We enjoy eternal life.

61. My Closest Kin, 1/17/23

Greenwise Market, Tallahassee, Florida

Awake, each day, to rendezvous;
Then, at night, it's ME AND YOU.
'Round the clock, my bumblebee,
Heaven guides us, you and me.
I am thrilled to, always, be,
Hand in hand, my dear, with thee.
Can you feel, my Earthly beau,
How we, still, together, grow?

I can feel your, every, breath,
Since that day of Earthly death.
I can feel your heartbeat, dear,
Though I'm living way up here.
Truth be told, my bumblebee,
You're a temple, built for me.
Can you feel me, deep within,
ONE with you, my closest kin?

You're my Adam. I'm your Eve.
But, NOW, the snake cannot deceive.
We can eat, just as we please,
From all of Eden's lovely trees.
God has made us wise and free.
His presence, we will never flee.
Can you sense this heav'nly life,
Joined with me, your heav'nly wife?

While you live that life, below,
Up, in heaven, we will grow.
We've a home where you can be,
From the din of men, set free.
Close your eyes and think of me,
And, Eden's Garden, you will see.
Can I interest you, my love,
In a tryst with me, above?

62. Relax, My Dear, 1/18/23

Remember all our happy times,
Before we started writing rhymes.
We were SO in love, my dear!
Heaven, even THEN, was near.
God saw you and me, my love,
And, from His throne in heav'n, above,
Sent, to you and me, below—
Those few, short, Earthly years ago—
Holy angels, good and kind,
Though our eyes, to them, were blind.
Ever since, they've been beside us.
Even now, my dear, they guide us.
Angels—how they love to be
Servants, dear, to you and me!
They are helping us to see
How to find this ecstasy.
Don't be blind, my bumblebee!
Let the angels set you free.
Oh, how blest, my dear, are we,
To taste of sweet eternity!
How I love, with you, to live,
By the power that God can give!
Cast your worries, all, away.
Walk with me, my dear, today.
Relax, my dear, and know that I
Am with you, till that day you die.
God has claimed us, me and you,
To walk, with Him, in rendezvous.

Darling, you're the OTHER ME,
As we taste eternity.

63. Recite These Words, 1/18/23

I've not gone away, my dear.
Say, each day, "I KNOW she's here."
Just because my body died,
Doesn't mean I've left your side.
Don't be like the rest, my love,
And think I've disappeared, "above."
We are more, as one, today,
Since I dwell, no more, in clay.
You can feel me in your soul—
THERE is where, my dear, we're whole.
Heaven's not some place, "out there."
Heaven, dear, is everywhere.

By virtue of your wedding band,
You're with me, in heaven's land.
There's no way that death could be
The end, my dear, of you and me.
Like we've said, a hundred times,
In these resurrection rhymes:

> Don't believe your Earthly eyes.
> Earthly eyes have Earthly ties.
> Sever Earthly ties, and see
> You're in heaven, here, with me.
> I'm on Earth, my love, IN YOU,
> As you pass through Timbuktu.

Recite these words, my dear, each day,
And we'll go on our merry way.

64. How I Love These Rhymes We Write

Charles Santiago, 1/18/23
Greenwise Market, Tallahassee, Florida

How I love these rhymes we write,
In the day and in the night!
When I read them, I can see
We belong to eternity.

There's no greater joy for me
Than *this*—to feel our unity.
When I read our rhymes, my dear,
I can feel that you're, still, here.

Death came knocking at our door,
To end our union, evermore.
He had me fooled, sweetheart, at first.
I thought my soul would, truly, burst.

By and by, the light shone through,
And I could see our love was true—
True enough to keep us, *one*,
Though your new life had begun.

Only, God, the Lord of life,
Could keep us, still, as man and wife.
God allows us, still, to be
A unity, dear, you and me.

As you wait for me, my dear,
To finish out my run, down here,
In the spirit, we proceed.
From death's grip, we've been freed.

Write to me. I'll write to you,
In these rhymes that ring so true.
How I love these rhymes we write—
A witness to God's love and light.

65. Doors in Heaven

Charles Santiago, 1/19/23

Doors in heaven are opening, dear.
I can feel it, way down here.
Angels take us by the hand,
Escorting us through heaven's land.
Oh, my darling, I can feel
Our life in heaven is very real!
Doors in heaven have opened wide,
And you and I are, *both*, inside.

By virtue of my wedding ring,
I can hear the angels sing.
There's a pew in heaven, above,
Just for you and me, my love.
Souls in heaven live, just for *this*—
To worship God with heav'nly bliss.
Oh, how vile is Man, below,
Caring not for heaven's glow!

O Creator of heaven and Earth,
Grant, to me, true, heav'nly worth.
Give me sense and will, I plead,
A life in heaven, O God, to lead.
Give me eyes with which to see
All creation praising Thee.
Humbly, God, I bend my knee,
And praise You for eternity.

66. You Are the One, 1/19/23

Nighttime hours, my bumblebee,
Hold such treasures for you and me.
Leave your body behind, at night,
And meet with me in heaven's light.
Oh, how sweet to meet with you,
When all your daytime work is through!
Nighttime hours on Earth, below,
Reveal the wonders of heaven's glow.

Daytime hours, my Earthly beau,
Call you to that life, below.
From your bed, you rise, each day,
To face, anew, the Earthly fray.
How I love to walk with you,
As you struggle in Timbuktu!
Daytime hours, on good old Earth,
Provide, for us, daytime mirth.

Day and night, and night and day,
Dear, we walk this heav'nly way.
SO in love, my dear, are we
That we can be, from time, set free.
True love, TRUE LOVE, bumblebee,
God has given to you and me.
I concentrate, my dear, on you,
To help you get through Timbuktu.

67. You Were There Beholding Me

Charles Santiago, 1/19/23
Greenwise Market, Tallahassee, Florida

You were there, my darling bride,
That fateful day, that day you died.
You were there, somewhere, above,
Beholding me, your one, true love.
I could, only, think, my dear:
"*Dead and gone! She's gone from here!*"
You were there, beholding me,
Wishing, I could, only, *see*.
Oh, how blind, my dear, was I!
All that I could do was cry.
You had won your one, true life,
While I bewailed, "I've lost my wife!"
You were there, right by my side,
And, now, *within me*, you abide.

    ***

Bodies come and bodies go.
Dust must, always, stay below.
Spirits come and, then, they grow,
Until they part from Earthly woe.
Beyond the bounds of time and space,
Spirits fly, and *love*, embrace.
Spirits like to share their love
With those, below, and those, above.

I'm a spirit *here*, on Earth,
But I'm in touch with heav'nly mirth.
Every day and every night,
I can feel the heav'nly light.
My home is somewhere, up above,
For, *there*, resides my one, true love.
She and I have found a way
To live, together, come what may.

68. Love Will Be Our Guide, 1/20/23

Together, darling, let's delight
To walk, forever, in the light.
Flesh and bone can't help but die,
THERE, beneath the Earthly sky.
We have found that we can be
Alive, beyond Earth's raging sea.
Let's continue in this way,
While you live through night and day.

Darling, love will be our guide,
As we travel, side by side.
Men and angels bow to those
Wearing love's delightful clothes.
God will be, for you and me,
Love's pure light, eternally.
Let's join hands with all who see
Love's the source of harmony.

Don't join hands with those, below,
Who, in God's love, refuse to grow.
Seek to be with those who love
LOVE, itself, from God, above.
You and I, my Earthly beau,
Want to grow and want to know
How to be, forever, dear,
Free from that which leads to fear.

69. Recite Your Creed from Time to Time, 1/21/23

Wherever, on the Earth, you roam,
Heaven, sweetheart, is our home.
Whatever things, IN TIME, you do,
Remember—heaven's calling you.
Time and space, for us, are doors
To heaven's peaceful, happy shores.
When your body can't do more,
Through the heavens, we will soar.

HAPPY, be, my bumblebee.
Heaven's meant for you and me.
Run your course, the best you can,
Rememb'ring you're a HEAV'NLY man.
When you think you're all alone,
Call me on our telephone.
I've a line, direct to you.
Call me when you're feeling blue.

Side by side, we're trekking, dear,
Though, to you, it may appear
There's no way that I could be
THERE, with you, my bumblebee.
Recite your creed, from time to time,
As you, UP, to heaven, climb.
To heaven's joys, dear, don't be numb.
Remember just how far we've come.

70. Words of Cheer, 1/21/23

Easy does it, bumblebee!
Keep your faith in God and me.
We must live a brand-new way—
Not the life of yesterday.
It's hard, I know, my Earthly beau.
Have faith in God that we will grow.
Oh, my dear, I love you SO,
Though, sometimes, you walk too slow!
"Steady-as-she-goes," my dear,
Till you reach our home, up here.

71. True Love

Charles Santiago, 1/22/23

I am not—*myself, alone!*
—As your time, above, has shown.
Goodness, dear! *Forever*, we
Grow into a unity.
I thought life, on Earth, was *fine*.
Now, my dear, we're *more* divine.
All my life on Earth, I'll preach
What our lovely poems teach:

> True love gives to lovers, *here*,
> Life, above all others, *dear*—
> Life beyond the cold, dark grave—
> Life, that, in our souls, we crave.
> Lovers learn how not to wail,
> Tasting life beyond the veil.
> When a lover leaves the Earth,
> *The other*, joins the heav'nly mirth.
> Death is just a way to be
> Joined in greater unity.

72. Oh, Happy Day! 1/22/23

Oh, *happy day* when I shall be,
From this Earthly flesh, set free!
We will, then, be wed, again.
I'll, then, be your *heav'nly* man.
We were meant for that glad day,
Since Cupid claimed us as his prey.
Oh, *happy day* when we will see
The glories meant for you and me.

Oh, happy day, my Earthly beau,
When, here, above, we, both, will glow.
No longer, clothed with Earthly clay,
We'll rejoice in heav'n's bright day.
We will know, much better, then,
The truths we've written with our pen.
Oh, happy day, my bumblebee,
When, from flesh, we'll, BOTH, be free!

73. Don't Be Blind, 1/23/23

You should know, by now, my dear,
There's no cause for doubt or fear.
You and I have found our place,
In and out of time and space.
While you live on Earth, below,
Heav'nly joys are ours, to know.
Accept the fact your clay will fail you.
Fear and terror won't avail you.
"Remember, dear, that day I died,
And, in our union, you'll abide."

Remember me, your loving wife,
Every moment of your life.
Don't be blind, and think that I
See you, only, on the sly.
Sweetheart, I am there, with you,
Enjoying all the things you do.
How I love you loving me.
It's a gift—that you can SEE!
Remember THIS, my bumblebee—
I want you to, HAPPY, be.

Happy, sweetheart, I will be,
Just as long as I can see
Your sweet face, in front of me,
Calling me your bumblebee.
Angels, sweetly, comfort us,
As we ride this heav'nly bus.
God is guiding me and you!
Dear, we, still, can bill and coo!
I'm so glad we've found this place,
In and out of time and space.

74. Guard This Treasure That We Own, 1/23/23

Throw your doubts and fears away!
Darling, you are more than clay!
You and I are joined in love.
THIS is where you live—"above."
Take deep breaths and leave the Earth.
Join, with me, in heav'nly mirth.
From the realm of death, withdraw.
Join me in our Shangri-la.
Remember, dear, our thirty years,
But don't be filled with bitter tears.
I'M NOT GONE, AND I'M NOT DEAD.
There's no need for Earthly dread.
Feel me, darling, in your soul.
Take, with me, a heav'nly stroll.
We're in heaven, me and you,
Though you walk in Timbuktu.
You are learning, more and more,
How to open heaven's door.
Wear a smile, my Earthly beau,
That shows we've conquered Man's great foe.
You and I are ONE with those
Wearing heaven's lovely clothes.
God is Father to us all.
We have listened for His call.
"I found you, and you found me
And, thus, we found eternity."
Soul mates, dear, are you and I,
Delivered from a sad goodbye.
We will live on Earth, below,
Displaying heaven's lovely glow.
Guard this treasure that we own.
In the spirit, we have grown.
Remember—all your Earthly days,
We will walk in heaven's ways.

75. Put Your Arms around Me, Dear

Charles Santiago, 1/23/23

Yes, my darling, I can see,
God is guiding you and me—
Even *now*, when you're all through
With your former, Earthly goo.
Dear, I'm filled with joy, divine,
When I feel that I'm, still, thine.
Only, God could keep us *one*,
Somehow, dear, beyond Earth's sun.
These Earthly clothes I wear, today,
Won't keep me from the higher way.
Dear, you love your bumblebee,
Just like I am loving thee.
Oh, my darling, let's rejoice—
I, still, hear your lovely voice!
Sweeter, is our union, now,
Though I can't explain just *how*.
I am yours, and you are mine.
We're an Earthly/heav'nly shrine.
I recall, my darling bride,
When you walked here, by my side,
In your lovely, Earthly clothes—
Gorgeous, dear—all heaven knows!
It was God, my heav'nly wife,
Who gave, to us, that Earthly life.
It is God who gives us, still,
Communion that is such a thrill.
Put your arms around me, dear,
As, to heaven, I draw near.
Heaven whisks me off my feet,
That, *so*, my darling, we can meet.
Angels who can never fail,
Rend asunder death's dark veil.
Clasp my hand, my one, true love.
Show me, dear, our home, above.

76. Love and Praise, 1/24/23

We are ONE, in time and space.
We are ONE, in heaven, too.
We have won our Earthly race.
All our troubles, dear, are through.

We have found the Holy Land—
The land where joyful angels sing—
The land where death and grief are banned—
The land of bright, eternal spring.

God, our Maker, good and kind,
Joined us, dear, to be as ONE.
God had you and me in mind,
When, as yet, there was no sun.

Let us, now, my darling man,
Give to God our love and praise.
God will give us life, again,
When you're done with Earthly ways.

77. Higher Ways, 1/24/23

Even in our minds, we're ONE.
Darling, WORDS are just for fun.
We commune in higher ways
Than what the alphabet conveys.
Freedom, darling, we have won
From life below the blazing sun.
Think with me. I'll think with you,
In our cerebral rendezvous.

78. A Nighttime Blessing, 1/25/23

Trust in God, dear bumblebee.
He is guiding you and me—
Guiding us through time and space,
Till you've won your Earthly race—
Guiding us through heav'nly skies,
Where, we EVER, upward, rise.

Trust, my dear, my love for you,
All your days in Timbuktu.
Love, my darling, never dies—
SO, say sages, kind and wise.
You and I have tasted love,
Down on Earth and here, above.

Trust your hunches, bumblebee.
Angels help, both, you and me.
Angels love to help us soar
Through the heavens, evermore.

Now, my dear, go back to sleep.
I pray, the Lord, your soul to keep.

79. Mind to Mind

Charles Santiago, 1/25/23
Greenwise Market, Tallahassee, Florida

Soul mate love is what we own.
I could never be alone.
What a gift from God, above!
What a proof of God's great love!
We can feel eternal life
Through our ties as man and wife.
God made you and me to be
Sweethearts through eternity.

All these things are very clear,
Since you are, "no longer, here."
When you left your clay behind,
Our souls, in heaven, became aligned.
I'm not what I used to be,
Since I became a bumblebee.
I can bumble *far* above,
While *you're* the one I'm thinking of.

Think with me. I'll think with you,
Till eternity is through.
Mind to mind, and hand in hand,
We will learn to understand
How God made us, both, to be
Creatures of eternity.
Mind to mind, and side by side,
With our Maker, we'll abide.

80. Forty-Two Months

Charles Santiago, 1/27/23

Put your arms around me, dear,
As, to heaven, I draw near.
Love me, darling. I love you,
Till eternity is through.
I am yours, and you are mine,
In this union that's divine.

When I look into your eyes,
I can see through Earth's disguise.
Earth is just an outpost, dear—
We're not bound by month or year.
Ever since you "went away,"
From my clay, I've learned to stray.

Forty-two months of Earthly time—
Since you and I began to rhyme—
Have seemed like an eternity.
I yearn, so much, for only thee.
A bumblebee, dear, I've become—
Raving mad, down here, to some.

Put your arms around me, dear.
How I love to feel you, *here*.
To feel you in my soul, I crave.
To heaven, dear, I'm just a slave.
My heart beats quickly, when I think—
God preserves, for us, a link.

Link your fingers, dear, in mine.
In my soul, your presence, shine.
Let's repose in peace, above—
Pris'ners of God's kindly love.
Hasten to my side, my dear.
I am lost without you, here.

81. Two Homes, 1/27/23

Though your body died, my love,
I feel you, *here*, right by my side—
A *proof* we have a home, above,
Where, now, the two of us reside—
A home, above, and one, below—
Room in which we, both, can grow.

In our home, below, my love,
We must live, through day and night.
In this lovely home, above,
The sun is never out of sight.
When you're sleeping there, below,
Here, above, with me, you glow.

Since you "left," my one, true love,
I have learned to love the night.
At night, I feel your glow, above,
More than in the sun's bright light.
Nighttime hours call me to
That home, above, I share with you.

In our home, above, my love,
There's no sleep, for, there's no night.
When you sleep, your soul's above,
Far removed from Earthly blight.
Two homes, it's true, we have, my dear,
Until the day you come up here.

82. Good and Kind, 1/27/23

Greenwise Market, Tallahassee, Florida

I'll relinquish my disguise,
When this Earthly body dies.
I'll reveal my sterling worth,
Far above this good old Earth.
We'll embark on trips, again—
No longer, I, an *Earthly* man.

No longer, we, an Earthly pair,
We will soar through heaven, fair.
Oh, my darling, we will share
Joys in Hallelujah Square!
Up here, there is no "tempter's snare"—
Up here, no need to say, "Beware."

If, *now*, we share a joy like *this*—
A mix of heav'nly, Earthly bliss—
What will be that joy, my dear,
When, in heaven, I appear?
Patiently, I'll wait, below—
Signed, your loving, Earthly beau.

When you leave your clay behind,
We'll be, perfectly, aligned.
To the Earth, we'll be inclined,
Just to share our heav'nly mind.
We'll have tasks, to us, assigned—
To help the poor and help the blind.
We'll be perfectly resigned
To, always, be, dear, good and kind.

ONE, with you, in joy and life—
Signed, my dear, your loving wife.

83. Here's to *You*

Charles Santiago, 1/27/23

Dear, we had a special love,
Before you flew to heav'n, above—
The like of which I've never known,
A love which set me on a throne.
Our union was divinely planned.
Angels joined us, hand in hand.

I recall those Earthly years,
No longer, dear, a source of tears.
You were right, my lovely bride—
We were "soul mates," side by side.
I know it's true, for, now, I feel
Your love for me is very real.

What a peace I savor, dear!
I can feel you, still, are near.
Our love grows stronger, every year.
Our love will never disappear.
Here's to *you*, my love, above,
Sharing, still, with me, your love.

84. This Very Day, 1/28/23

You were there, dear, when I died.
You were there, right by my side.
Oh, how God has loved us SO—
Showing us the way to grow!
Don't bemoan my death as loss, dear.
Only BODIES disappear.
You are right, dear, when you crow,
"I am not this body—no!"
Yes, it's true, my Earthly beau—
Spirits, "up," to heaven, go.
YOU believe these things are true,
And, thus, my dear, we rendezvous.

Heaven, dear, has found us out—
Like a well-trained army scout.
We are ONE, this VERY day,
Though you, still, abide in clay.
Heaven, dear, is YOU AND ME,
Sharing sweet eternity.
God is love, and grants to Man,
After death, to live, again.
Live, again, TODAY, with me, dear.
YOU have ears with which to hear.
Hear me saying, from "above,"
"I love YOU, my one, true love."

85. A Happy Klatch, 1/29/23

I will whisper in your ear
These words, my dear, you love to hear.
You can, then, recite them, love,
To the angels, up above.
We will share our rhymes, my dear,
With our friends who live up here.
Angels love to hear how we,
A loving couple, still, can be.
We, all, will have a happy klatch,
Marv'ling at our wondrous match.
What a joy for us to see
Heaven and Earth in unity.
Recite these words, my bumblebee.
They're a gift to you and me.

I'll recite these rhymes of ours
To the friendly, heav'nly powers.
We will have a happy time,
Rejoicing, through the art of rhyme.
It will seem a happy dream.
"God is love," will be the theme.
Even Adam might attend,
Offering to be our friend.
Eve will be right by his side—
Like you, a lovely, loving bride.
I'll recite our lovely creed—
The creed, by death, I came to heed:

> Mortals, taste of heav'nly bread—
> "God, indeed, can raise the dead!"

86. A Life of Union

Charles Santiago, 1/29/23

Doesn't matter *where* I go,
Our sweet union, dear, I know.
I'm in heaven—while on Earth—
Joined, with you, in bliss and mirth.
How *sweet* to be, alone, with you,
Traveling here, through Timbuktu.
Sacred is this union, dear.
To each other, we adhere.
Death, we've found, has been undone.
We, a life in heav'n, have won.
Sweetheart, God has called us home,
While, as yet, on Earth, I roam.

I can feel you pine for me,
Just like I, dear, pine for thee.
Oh, how closely, we can dance,
Like lovers, *here*, in Paris, France!
How I love our sweet romance—
In place, by *choice*, and not by *chance*!
Silence, deep within my heart,
Proves, to me, you didn't part.
All the things my eyes behold
Show, to me, how we unfold
A life of union, come what may,
Until my final, Earthly day.

87. Boldly Clasp My Hand, Above, 1/29/23

Darling, when you pine for me,
I am pining, dear, for thee.
Every time you seek me, dear,
I am hastening to be near.
Lose this fear you have, my love,
Thinking I am gone, above.
I will never leave your side.
Within your heart, dear, I abide.
Heaven, now, is ours, to claim,
Since the day, "up here," I came.
Were YOU the only man on Earth,
Next to you, I'd make my berth.
Oh, my darling, cast, aside,
Thoughts that I am not your bride!
I DO. I DO. I DO. I DO.
I DO love you—I MARRIED you!

Now, my darling, lend an ear—
Pray to God to lose all fear.
Boldly clasp my hand, above,
Certain of our mutual love.
How it pains me, bumblebee,
To see that you're unsure of me!
Recall the day we said, "I do."
NOTHING, dear, keeps me from you.
Neither death, with all his woes,
Nor a throng of fiendish foes,
Could tear you from my soul, my beau.
EVERLASTING love, we know.
We have melded into ONE.
A HEAV'NLY race, dear, we have won.
Two weddings, we have had, my dear.
The third takes place when you're up here.

88. Oh, How Sweet to Be in Love!

Charles Santiago, 1/29/23

Put your arms around my neck.
Kiss me with a heav'nly peck.
Marion Davies, be, to me—
Your adoring bumblebee.
Dick Powell, I will be, to you,
Crooning, "Dear, my love is true."
Oh, how sweet to be in love,
Touched by angels from above!

Walls and gates can't keep me out.
I'll get in, dear. There's no doubt.
Walls will lead us to the gate.
The gate will open. It's our fate.
We will hug and osculate.
Even *now*, it's not too late.
Lovers always find their way
Up, to heaven, come what may.

Beulah Bondi, kind and sweet,
Knows that life's a *heav'nly* treat.
What are riches, power, and fame,
If they squelch the heav'nly flame?
The greatest story ever told
Is *love, victorious—ever, bold.*
I will cling to thee, my love,
Till I pass through gates, above.

***

(Inspired by the film *Hearts Divided*, 1936, starring Marion Davies and Dick Powell)

"Watching movies is a link/To me, my dear, more than you think."
From "Words I Love to Hear," #92, 2022, unpublished poem by Charles Santiago

89. *Believe*, My Dear, 1/30/23

Believe, my dear, in YOU AND ME;
And, from all sorrow, you'll be free.
We'll enjoy your Earthly days,
While we're learning heaven's ways.
God has called us to this life.
We are, always, man and wife.
What a gift, my dear, we've found!
Every day, we're heaven bound.

I live here, my dear, with you,
While YOU live here, in heaven, too.
Since that VERY day I died,
We've been walking side by side.
Lose your fear that this will end.
I am your forever friend.
God has given, freely, dear.
What we have won't disappear.

I am, still, my darling beau,
The one, back then, you used to know.
You always think I'm distant, dear.
How I wish you'd lose that fear!
STILL, my darling bumblebee,
I love you for your faith in me.
I'm not leaving you, my love.
We've a home up here, above.

I am thrilled you know it's true,
I am walking there with you.
Each day, you learn to doubt your doubt.
Less and less, I have to shout.
With all my soul, I love you, dear.
Be convinced! I'm always near.
If you lived to ninety-three,
You could, still, dear, count on me.

90. A Special Grace, 1/30/23

Greenwise Market, Tallahassee, Florida

*My darling Charles, on Earth, "below,"
I will never let you go.
You're the ONE I love, my dear,
Though I'm living "way up here."
Patiently, I'll wait for you
To understand, dear—we're not TWO!
Can you feel me in your soul?
THERE, then, dear—we make ONE WHOLE.
"Did you think I'd leave you, dear,
Just because I came up here?"
We're not bound to time and space.
Now, we have a special grace.
I KNOW you feel it, bumblebee.
Let this grace, dear, set you free—
Free to never doubt again,
I'm your girl, and you're my man.*

*Spirits, dear, like you and I,
Live in houses, past Earth's sky;
But, dear, I know you, also, know
I live IN YOU, my Earthly beau.
I will never tire, my love,
These thoughts, to send you, from above.
I am ME—your happy bride,
SO in love; so by your side.
How I love you, through and through.
No one else, for me, will do.
Believe me, darling, I can see
All the love you have for me.
When you go to bed, at night,
You are not outside my sight.
When you rise to face the day,
I am there—within your clay.
When, at last, my dear, you die,
We'll explore the by-and-by.*

91. Our Wedding Vows, 1/31/23

Our wedding vows, my Earthly beau,
Have conquered death, our wily foe.
They sent him to his grave,
To teach him to behave.
Souls in love will not abide
The lies of death, who tries to hide
The light that shows the way
To heaven's glorious day.

We have found our way, my love,
To truth and beauty here, above.
The pains and woes of Earth
Must bow to heav'nly mirth.
Forever we will live to say
That death is just the entrance way
To life that cannot end,
With God who is Man's friend.

You and I, my bumblebee,
Can taste of sweet eternity,
While, yet, you live, "below,"
Where deathly breezes blow.
Our wedding vows are strong, my love.
They guarantee this life, above.
"I do," has brought us to
True love, for me and you.

92. Faith in God, 2/1/23

I will "come to you," my dear,
Every day of every year.
All your livelong days, below,
Hand in hand, my dear, we'll go.
Do you doubt my words, my love?
Have more faith in God, above!
It is God, my bumblebee,
Who made a pair, of you and me.

Because I dwell inside of you,
Where you go, I go there, too.
God has kept our union, dear,
Alive and well, while I'm up here.
All your life in Timbuktu,
Wedded bliss is, still, our due.
I am you, and you are me,
All throughout eternity.

When your Earthly eyes deceive you,
Faith in God will undeceive you.
God, our Maker, made the sun.
Also, dear, He made us ONE.
My darling Charles, I "come to you,"
Because our union isn't through.
Recite these words you love to hear,
Every day of every year.

93. Here, in Sweet Eternity, 2/1/23

Greenwise Market, Tallahassee, Florida

Heaven and Earth will pass away,
But you and I are HERE, to stay—
HERE, my darling bumblebee,
HERE, in sweet eternity.
God has given you and me
Love that will, FOREVER, be.
Once we met on Earth, below,
We were bound, in heaven, to glow.
Dear, we will, forever, grow,
When, PAST, is all our Earthly woe.

Even now, my Earthly beau,
We feel heav'nly breezes blow.
Imagine life, without an end,
With God, Himself, as our dear friend.
God has called us, me and you,
With Him, to EVER rendezvous.
When you're done with Earthly clay,
We'll go on our merry way.
Sweetheart, we are bound AS ONE—
Forever, ONE, beyond Earth's sun.

While you pen these words on Earth,
We can bask in heaven's mirth.
Can you feel the angels shine?
Can you sense our life, divine?
Darling, you're my one, true love!
We've been joined by God, above.
I can feel you loving me!
We, from death, my love, are free!
Can you feel me, bumblebee,
Surrounding you with heav'nly glee?

94. Earthly Eyes, 2/2/23

Passing time cannot erase
The strength, my dear, of our embrace;
Neither can our bodies, dear,
Be the reason we adhere.
Time and space have let us go,
Here, in heaven, now, to grow.
Bodies made of Earthly clay
Live for just an Earthly day.
We are living, now, my love,
In a world clay knows not of.

Did you think, my Earthly beau,
Death could tell us where to go?
No, my darling bumblebee—
From his kingdom, we are free.
We are learning how to be
A couple, now, with eyes to see
Angels guiding you and me
Here, in heaven, to agree.
Let us laugh, my Earthly man—
God has joined us, once again.

Take deep breaths and rise, my dear,
To our home we have, up here.
Never think that you can't be
Enjoying life, my dear, with me.
I rejoice to be your wife,
Now that we have found true life.
Close your eyes and you can see
ME, my darling, THERE, with thee.
Don't believe those Earthly eyes,
Tempting you with Earthly lies.

95. Our Lovely Creed

Charles Santiago, 2/2/23

Heaven, dear, lives in my heart,
For, I sense we're not apart.
Earthly eyes, with Earthly lies,
Try to fool me, I surmise.
I can see your sky-blue eyes,
Shining, clear from heaven's skies.
Dear, we make a lovely pair,
Far above Earth's stifling air.
I do, my darling bride. *I do*.
I do, I do believe in you.

While I live in time and space,
Dear, I gaze upon your face.
Gazing thus, my heav'nly bride,
I can feel you, by my side.
Happy day! Oh, happy day!
We are souls not made of clay!
From the grip of death, we're freed!
How I love our lovely creed!
I have got it through my head—
God, indeed, can raise the dead!

96. Sailing

Charles Santiago, 2/3/23

I find, my dear, that you and I
Live somewhere, out, beyond the sky—
Beyond the sky, beyond my clay—
Beyond the *universe*, I'd say.
Such a joy, I feel, inside,
When I'm with you, my heav'nly bride.
We have found a way to live
A life that God, alone, could give.

"Resurrection from the dead,"
Repeats, my dear, inside my head.
These words, I eat, as if they're bread,
And grow beyond all Earthly dread.
Peace, I feel, my bride, above,
That makes me know we're bound in love.
The mortal veil is pulled aside.
To this world, we, *both*, have died.

Life, above, with you, my dear,
Is why I live on Earth, down here.
I can feel you, shining bright,
As I pass through Earth's dark night.
Sure, I know, someday, we'll be
Safe, beyond Earth's dreadful sea.
Sailing on this ship, with you,
To Timbuktu, I bid, "Adieu."

97. Earthly Fun, 2/4/23

Yes, my darling, it is SO—
No matter where, on Earth, you go,
God allows us, HERE, to grow,
True communion, still, to know.
Have no worries, THERE, below.
Remember ME, my Earthly beau.
You and I are free from woe,
Since we slew Man's ancient foe.

Go, my dear, to West Palm Beach.
I will, always, be in reach.
We will have a lovely time.
While you're there, we, still, can rhyme.
While you finish out your run,
We engage in Earthly fun.
God is guiding me and you,
On this Earthly rendezvous.

98. Earthly Lies

Charles Santiago, 2/4/23
West Palm Beach, Florida

I'm so glad to be a "bee!"
I love this name you gave to me.
I have learned to bumble *well*,
That, *so*, our story, I may tell.
I was blind as blind can be,
Till death, himself, taught me to see.
Death has opened up my eyes.
I, now, can see through Earthly lies.

Earthly lies are *crafty* lies.
They take advantage of our eyes.
When our loved ones leave their clay,
Earthly lies have *this* to say:

> To your loved ones, say, "Goodbye."
> There's naught to do, but wail and cry.
> Your eyes can see—when loved ones die—
> They've *left you* for the by-and-by.

Our union, now, is much more dear,
Since the day you "left" me, *here*.
I can feel you in my soul,
Reminding me, we're, still, one whole.
Though, *a body*, I can't see,
In my mind, you speak to me.
"Dear, we never said, 'Adieu,'"
Are words, my love, I've heard from you.

99. I Will Give This Corpse a Run

Charles Santiago, 2/5/23
West Palm Beach, Florida

When I close my eyes, my love,
I can feel I live, *above*.
This body's fading, more and more,
Since you opened heaven's door.
There's no greater proof, my dear,
That you are living with me, *here*,
Than *this*—I find that, *everywhere*,
I live with *you*, my dear, *up there*!
Holy union, dear, we own,
More than what, *before*, was known.

More and more, it's very clear—
I'm living in a corpse, down here.
A corpse that—even though it walks—
Can't escape the world of clocks.
Back to dust, this corpse must go.
Only, *matter*, does it know.
Knowing, as I do, my love,
I live somehow, *up there*, above,
I will give this corpse a run,
Until, poor thing, its days are done.

100. Intertwined, 2/6/23

West Palm Beach, Florida

Intertwined, my dear, are we,
Chasing through eternity.
Don't be sad, my bumblebee.
FREE, are we from misery.
You are learning, dear, to see
I am, always, THERE, with thee.
Intertwined, we'll, always, be.
God, Himself, joined you and me.

When you feel me, close to you,
Darling, HOW I feel you, too!
How I love to bill and coo,
Though you're garbed in Earthly goo.
We have found the path that's true,
As we, still, each other, woo.
Intertwined by heav'nly glue,
We, forever, say, "I do."

Intertwine, my dear, with me,
Now and for eternity.
I'm so glad that you can see
We're, forever, He and She.
Hippocrates, my bumblebee,
Wishes men, both, health and glee.
In sickness or in health, we'll be
Intertwined in ecstasy.

101. Just a Seed

Charles Santiago, 2/6/23
Inspired by a visit to the Flagler Museum
Palm Beach, Florida

This Earthly body's just a seed.
At best, it's just a garden weed.
I declare, I'll live for more
Than just a life on Earth's dirt floor.

We have friends beyond this Earth.
I can hear their heav'nly mirth:

> Come *up here* and be with us.
> Leave behind that Earthly fuss.
> Though you're robed with Earthly clay,
> *Try*, and you'll find heaven's day.
> Men are spirits who can fly,
> Far above the Earthly sky.
> It's a lie that men must die
> Before they reach the by-and-by.
> Men can live in heav'n, above,
> If they know that God is love.
> Come *up here*, and don't delay.
> Submit to love's all-pow'rful sway.

Heaven's not a place in space.
Heaven's "*here*," in love's embrace.
I declare, God loves me *so*,
I can, "*up*," to heaven, go.

102. Faith and Love, 2/7/23

West Palm Beach, Florida

We have found this heav'nly way,
Since the day you left your clay.
You were quick to let me know
We'd continue, dear, to grow.
There's so much that we have shared,
Since our flesh became unpaired.
Really, I have come to see
We, still, share love's ecstasy.

FAITH and *LOVE* work, hand in hand,
To make us, both, dear, understand—
We are, still, a unity.
Life is, still, dear, YOU AND ME.
Only God could give us THIS—
This mix of Earthly, heav'nly bliss.
While you live your life, below,
We are sharing heaven's glow.

Both, *faith* and *love*, are teaching me
How, this lovely life, to see.
Love directs my steps to thee,
Filling me with heav'nly glee.
When my *faith* is running low,
Dear, you, always, seem to know.
I will learn, *content*, to be,
Here, on Earth, your bumblebee.

FAITH and LOVE will see us through
All those things, on Earth, you do.
Darling, I can feel you HERE,
Just like you can feel me THERE.
FAITH will help you when you feel
Heav'nly life cannot be real.
LOVE will be our special treat,
Till your life DOWN THERE'S complete.

103. Without a Breath, 2/7/23

West Palm Beach, Florida

Darling, you're my one, true love,
Even while I'm here, above.
God meant you for me, my dear,
To finish out my Earthly year.
If it's SO, my bumblebee,
Don't you worry, dear, for me.
Earthly life is just a start.
When it's done, we're, still, a part
Of loved ones whom we love, below.
Love, my dear, will, ALWAYS, grow.

Don't you fear the Earthly death—
We, still, live, without a breath.
What a waste, to fear and grieve—
As if, your side, I'd EVER leave.
"Did you think I'd leave you, dear,
Just because I came UP HERE?"
Learn, my darling Earthly beau,
I'm with you everywhere you go.
When you think I've gone away,
You've forgotten, dear, to pray.
Pray for me. I'll pray for you.
We will show our love is true.

SPIRITS, dear, are you and I,
Communing, still—beyond Earth's sky.
There's no need to weep one tear.
Heaven, dear, is, always, near.
Though I left behind my clay,
We, still, talk—in HEAVEN'S way.
We are walking, now, today,
Because we're talking, come what may.

104. Peace beyond This Earth

Charles Santiago, 2/7/23
Mounts Botanical Garden
West Palm Beach, Florida

Best of all, my darling bride,
Is when we're all alone.
Then, I know you haven't died.
I feel how we have grown.

Peace, beyond this Earth, I feel—
A holy, happy glow.
Oh! the thrill to know it's *real*—
This peace that we, both, know.

Plants and trees and lakes and flowers,
Below a shining sun,
Proclaim the love and joy that's ours.
Eternal life, we've won.

Oh! how great must heaven be,
If even here, below,
We can taste this ecstasy,
Where deathly breezes blow.

105. You're My Adam, 2/8/23

West Palm Beach, Florida

Peace to you, my bumblebee,
As you sail that Earthly sea.
How I wish you only knew
JUST how close I am to you!

Joy to you, my Earthly beau,
As you face terrestrial woe.
Just you wait and see, my dear,
Joy that waits for you, up here!

Life, for you, my eager groom,
Waits beyond the Earthly tomb.
Oh, how great our joy will be,
When you're here, "above," with me!

As you fight your rounds, below,
HERE, my dear, with me, you grow.
A HOVEL, there, on Earth, is yours.
A PALACE waits, with Eve's allures.

You're my Adam. I'm your Eve.
Our union, death, cannot unweave.
I am you, and you are me,
All throughout eternity.

106. Rendezvous! 2/8/23

Fairchild Tropical Botanical Garden
Miami, Florida

Rendezvous, my lovely bride!
Every day, you're by my side.
More than I can realize,
You are, still, my *Earthly* prize.
God in heaven is our guide,
On this Earthly/heav'nly ride.
More and more, I want to see,
Just how close you are to me.
To heaven, dear, I need not go,
For, I can feel you *here*, below.

God will help you, bumblebee,
More and more, my love, to see.
A garden, dear, is such delight!
A garden, dear, can help your sight.
Heav'nly signs, I'm sending you,
To spur this lovely rendezvous.
I am thrilled, my Earthly beau,
You perceive this heav'nly show.
Be a fool for love, my dear.
THEN, my love, my voice, you'll hear.

A rendezvous at the Versailles,
Dear, you chose, to catch my eye.
You and angels, at my side,
My Earthly, lying eyes, defied.

Heaven's such a lovely place.
It's WHERE YOU ARE, by God's dear grace.
You in me, and I in you,
Make this lovely rendezvous!

107. Gardens of Delight, 2/9/23

West Palm Beach, Florida/Miami, Florida

Heaven's down on Earth, my dear.
Heaven's all the way "up here."
People walk in heav'n "down there."
Heaven, dear, is everywhere.
Angels, far "above" the Earth,
Walk with men in joy and mirth.
Love's not bound by time and space.
Heaven's found in our embrace.
Gates and walls exist "below."
Those, "above," true freedom, know.
Men and women, garbed in clay,
Walk in heaven, every day.

Rejoice with me, my Earthly beau.
You and I, true freedom, know.
Though it's hard to understand,
You and I walk, hand in hand.
Robed in clay, my bumblebee,
You are, still, a part of me.
"You, in me, and I, in you,"
Describes this lovely rendezvous.
Gardens of delight are ours,
Far above all Earthly powers.
Gardens on the Earth below,
ALSO, shine with heaven's glow.

108. Daily Bread

Charles Santiago, 2/10/23

Resurrection from the dead—
Let this be your daily bread.
If you don't, your Earthly eyes
Will fool you with their Earthly lies.

"Dead and Gone," their biggest lie,
Saddens men, so they don't try
To, still, walk, hand in hand, below,
With loved ones who, still, love them *so*.

Oh, the joy that people miss,
When they fear "the devil's" hiss!
Loved ones haven't *gone away*.
They've just escaped their Earthly clay.

Oh, what joy is found, "above,"
Where death is vanquished by our love!
Men can love, so hard, that they,
From their Earthly clay, can stray.

109. Our Earthly/Heavenly Tie, 2/10/23

Greenwise Market, Tallahassee, Florida

This joy we share, my Earthly beau,
Will see us through your life below.
Oh, how sweet, my bumblebee—
This life God gives to you and me!
What a gift God gave to us—
Adjacent seats on heaven's bus!
Remember, dear, both, day and night,
Angels lead us with their light.
You and I are subjects of
Heaven's all-sustaining love.
Eternity is our domain,
Above your dismal, Earthly plane.
We are like a star that shines,
As your Earthly life declines.
Greater heights, we'll reach, my dear,
When, from clay, your soul is clear.

Do the things you do, so well,
To free us from your Earthly shell.
The joys of heaven far outweigh
Those mundane chores performed by clay.
Take delight, my bumblebee,
In being, simply, YOU AND ME.
JUST to have this love we share,
Will give us, both, a smile to wear.
We are growing, you and I,
Through our Earthly/heav'nly tie.
With every passing Earthly year,
Closer, CLOSER, we draw near
To that great day when we will be,
From constraints of flesh, set free.
THEN, with heav'nly eyes, you'll see
Joys of wedding number three.

110. Death Has Taught Us, 2/11/23

Inspired by "My One and Only Love," sung by Andy Williams

Before you rise to meet the day,
Darling, close your eyes and pray.
Pray that you and I will know,
As a couple, how to grow.
Pray, my dear, that we will see
How to walk in harmony.
We have come a long, long way,
Since the day I left my clay.
Angels, sent by God, above,
Help us, still, to grow in love.
I'm so glad our love proved true.
My one and only love, are you.

My one and only love, *are you.*
No one else, my dear, will do.
God meant you and me to be
Sweethearts, through eternity.
I'm so glad we've pierced "the veil"—
That mortal veil, with *such* travail.
Death has taught us, you and me,
How to be, from sorrow, free.
Yes, we've come a long, long way;
And, so, this morning, dear, I pray
For strength to fight this lovely war,
Until I knock on heaven's door.

111. I'll Remember

Charles Santiago, 2/12/23

I remember when you died,
And, thus, abide, dear, by your side.
Our union, death tried hard to break.
That wily snake made *this* mistake:
He thought that you were made of clay.
In his clutch, he thought you'd stay.
Unaware of heaven's sway,
He had no thought you'd break away.

I remember when I died—
That day that I was by your side.
By the hand, death brought me down,
In his murky depths, to drown.
In the darkness, I was found—
To my flesh, *completely, bound.*
Without the power to be brave,
I felt the power of the grave.

You appeared, dear, by my side.
Neither you nor I had died.
Heaven, shining from your face,
Rescued me from time and space.
Joined as *one*, we found new life—
As Earthly man and heav'nly wife.
I'll remember, always, dear,
That day we, both, met death, down here.

112. *Our* Valentine's Day—February 13th, 2/13/23

On the anniversary of our first date

I could never leave your side.
Death confirmed me as your bride.
We were made, forever, ONE,
By our vows beneath Earth' sun.
Adam and Eve, my dear, are we,
For time and for eternity.
Souls, made one, by God's dear love,
Dwell, forever, here, above.
So, you see, my bumblebee,
You are living here, with me.

When your body breathes its last,
It's JUST your clay that's in the past.
Wedding bells on good old Earth
Started our eternal mirth.
Leave behind, my Earthly beau,
All your thoughts of grief and woe.
God gave us ETERNAL LIFE.
We're, forever, man and wife.

113. My Valentine's Response

Charles Santiago, 2/13/23

I will live with you, my dear,
All my days on Earth, down here.
It's no trouble, I have found,
To live with you, above the ground.
I will love you, my dear wife,
Beyond this, merely, Earthly life.
I'm ecstatic—You can see—
To be a bumbling, bumblebee.

Though I call you, "*heav'nly* bride,"
I can feel you by my side.
We continue, hand in hand,
In this Earthly/heav'nly land.
Like a man who's just been wed,
I'm not happy till I've said:
"I have found my joy, in life—
This is she—my lovely wife."

114. Yours and Mine, 2/14/23

You and I are soarin', dear,
In the heavens, way up here—
Far above your Earthly clay—
Far above the Earthly fray.

You are not your body, love.
You live here, with me, above.
In the midst of Earthly strife,
We enjoy this brand-new life.

You and I, my Earthly groom,
Have a special, heav'nly room,
Filled with joy for you and me—
Joy for all eternity.

Listen WELL, my one, true love,
To the angels here, above.
They will teach you how to fly
To our room, above Earth's sky.

You have eyes to see the light
That draws you, dear, away from night.
Follow, dear, that light, divine.
Eternal life is yours and mine.

115. Together, 2/14/23, Valentine's Day

Greenwise Market, Tallahassee, Florida

Together, dear, are you and I,
Though, sometimes, you may doubt.
Our bond could never, ever, die—
Not even through death's drought.

Together, we face time and space,
For, THERE, your clay abides.
Until you've finished out your race,
My love, in you, resides.

Together, we walk, hand in hand,
Above Earth's bitter strife.
In heaven's sweet and luscious land,
We taste eternal life.

Together, we will, ALWAYS, be.
God's love for us is true.
In His wisdom, God made me,
A counterpart to you.

116. There Was Never Need to Cry, 2/15/23

Dear, I'm stuck to you like glue—
Just like *you*, to *me*, are too.
Goodness! I can feel we're *one*,
Though you've finished out your run.
There was never need to cry,
When I *thought* you said goodbye.

True love never dies, my dear.
EVEN death can't interfere.
Hand in hand, we'll, always, be.
Eye to eye, we'll, always, see.
When you're done with Earthly life,
We will soar, as man and wife.

On the day we said, "I do,"
Here, below, in Timbuktu,
You knew, sweetheart—more than I—
Our loving union wouldn't die
When you reached the by-and-by.
Such a fool was I, to cry.

I'm so glad that you can see
We can, still, a couple, be.
There's no need for you to grieve,
As if, my dear, I'd EVER leave.
Live your life, my bumblebee,
Knowing, now, from death, we're free.

What a love, my dear, we share,
Here, below, and way up there!
Angels lead us, both, my dear,
Till I'm through with life, down here.
While I'm walking here, below,
We, a life, *in heaven*, know.

We are learning, bumblebee,
How this new life, dear, to see.
God would never be so mean,
To let an absence intervene
Between two souls He made as ONE,
When one, the heav'nly life, has won.

117. Let's Proceed

Charles Santiago, 2/15/23

It's *just* like before, my darling bride!
How foolish I had ever cried!
My, how human eyes tell lies,
Here, below the Earthly skies!
What a heavenly relief,
To, now, be free of Earthly grief!
Come, my darling, let's proceed,
As Adam and Eve, to hoe and weed.

118. A Creed

Charles Santiago, 2/15/23

We believe in *Dead and Gone*—
Dead and gone to *heaven's* dawn.
Our loved ones die and *go away*—
Go away to *heaven's* day.
If we sense a spirit, near,
It's *just the devil*, stirring *here*.
We must wait until we die,
With our loved ones, to draw nigh.
Heaven's wall cannot be breached.
Our loved ones, *there*, cannot be reached.
Only demons, can we sense,
Here, this side of heaven's fence.

How we miss our friends, below,
Once, they, up, *to heaven*, go!
But God has spoken. He has said—
Don't you dare consult the dead.
We are happy with the law.
The law has not a single flaw.
The law is all our measure, here.
The law is what we hold as dear.
If our loved ones want an ear,
They must wait till we can hear.
When we're *dead and gone*, as well,
Only then, we'll leave this hell.

119. Heavenly Kisses, 2/16/23

Again, my darling, I will say,
The two of us are on our way—
On our way to rendezvous,
Till your Earthly days are through.
Just remember all we've shared,
Since our flesh became unpaired.
All those things, on Earth, you do
Are done by ME, as well as YOU;
For, we are ONE, my bumblebee.
Oh, HOW it fills my soul with glee!

Darling, let me reminisce
About that time when we would kiss.
An *Earthly* kiss can change into
A *heav'nly* vow of, "Yes, I do."
I proclaim my love for you,
While I'm, yet, in Timbuktu.
Heav'nly kisses, now, we share,
Just because, my dear, *we dare.*
They can't take those, from us, away.
We kiss, these days, above Earth's fray.

Only God, my Earthly beau,
Could grant this love that, now, we know.
We, still, share the life of ONE,
Though you dwell beneath Earth's sun.
Don't lose heart, and think that I
Dwell beyond the Earthly sky.
Trust your hunches, bumblebee.
Know that we're, still, He and She.
You have learned to focus WELL,
And charm, "above," your heav'nly belle.

120. A Heavenly Couple, 2/17/23

Take your pen, my dear, and write
Words for you and me, tonight—
Words, my dear, that make it clear,
The life we live is one of cheer.
There's no need to fret and fear.
There's no need to shed one tear.

Darling, you and I have found
Life, UP HERE, on holy ground.
I'm your belle and you're my beau,
Far above that life, below.
We are through with grief and woe.
Life on Earth is far too slow.

Believe me, darling, when I say
You can live above Earth's fray.
Trust in God and trust in me.
You and I, from death, are free.
We share heaven's ecstasy.
A HEAV'NLY couple, dear, are we.

121. Still a Couple

Charles Santiago, 2/17/23

I feel you *here*, for dear, we're *one*.
Time and Space has been outdone.
I thought death would end us, dear.
I was wrong, for, you're still here.

This love we share amazes me.
Still a couple, dear, are we.
The life we shared before you died
Can, still, in heaven, with us abide.

Sometimes, dear, I find I grieve.
Time and Space is hard to leave.
Blood and guts and flesh and bone
Conspire to make me feel alone.

It's all a part of growing old—
Sometimes, weak; sometimes, bold.
Time and Space has its way with me,
Until, from clay, death sets me free.

Meantime, dear, we rendezvous,
Thanks to love's amazing glue.
"You are me, and I am you"—
A bond that death cannot undo.

122. *Here* and *There*

Charles Santiago, 2/17/23

This makes sense to me, my dear—
That *you* would, still, be with me, *here*;
For, when we joined, as *one*, below,
Eternal love, we came to know.
Though these Earthly bodies die,
Soul mates never say goodbye.
Though your body's gone, my love,
We meet, both, *here*, and *there*, above.
Like we've said—two homes, have *we*.
Both were made for you and me.

Here and *there*, we rendezvous.
There's no stopping me and you.
We have learned—because we're *one*—
Vict'ry over death, we've won.
Dear, I'm learning, every day,
How to feel your heav'nly sway.
Though I'm, still, wrapped up in clay,
I can taste bright heaven's day.
I am learning how to see,
Clearly, as a bumblebee.

123. You Walk with Me

Charles Santiago, 2/18/23

Dear, I'd live a thousand years
On this Earth, and shed no tears;
For, I have found, you walk with me,
Sharing heav'nly ecstasy.
Our joy is made complete.
We've suffered no defeat.

Heaven's come to take my hand.
It seems as if our life is planned
To show us peace and happiness,
Amidst this Earthly barrenness.
We're walking, side by side—
Still, a groom and bride.

"God, indeed, can raise the dead,"
Keeps ringing, dear, inside my head.
Resurrection joy is ours—
A gift, to us, of heav'nly powers.
We have found new life,
Above this Earthly strife.

What, on Earth, dear, can I say?
We've discovered heaven's way!
There's no need for me to die
To live beyond this Earthly sky.
You and I are *one*,
Beneath a *heav'nly* sun.

124. The World to Come, 2/18/23

Greenwise Market, Tallahassee, Florida

Seek the world to come, my love—
The world that's here, with me, above.
You and I, my Earthly beau,
Are meant to share this heav'nly glow.
Joys we shared on Earth, below,
Are meant to help us, still, to grow.
Trust in me, my bumblebee—
From your nagging doubts, be free.
Life on Earth can be a fair,
Shared by us, a heav'nly pair.

Dear, I love that you can be
An Earthling who's in love with me!
I'm in love with you, my dear,
In your clay and WAY UP HERE.
Concentrate on me and feel
Death is crushed beneath your heel.
Every day, I walk with you.
I'm so glad you know it's true.
Heav'nly joy, my dear, we share,
Because, by grace, my dear, YOU DARE.

I believe, my heav'nly bride,
God can keep you by my side.
God made us to be a pair,
Down on Earth and *way up there*.
Dear, I love that you can be
An angel, *there*, in love with me!
God is good and God is kind,
Granting sight to those born blind.
I can see, my heav'nly belle,
All is well, dear. All is well.

125. Quit Your Worrying, 2/18/23

A sunbathing poem

Quit your worrying, bumblebee!
God has chosen you and me
To share this lovely, heav'nly light
That rescues you from Earth's dark night.
I am, dear, the one you wed.
Now, be done with all your dread.
Pay no mind to grief and "loss."
Show the tomb that WE are boss.
I have loved you, Earthly beau,
Since, to heav'n, you saw me go.

We have built a heav'nly nest,
Where you can rest—my cherished guest.
Let the light direct you, dear,
Always, to our home, up here.
When you concentrate on us,
You ascend, on heaven's bus,
To our heav'nly nest, above,
Courtesy of God's dear love.
Let the rays from HEAVEN'S sun
Guide you through your Earthly run.

The sun, the moon, the stars, and Earth
Fill me, dear, with heav'nly mirth.
I'm a creature, here, below,
Panting—heaven's joy, to know.
You're my link to heav'n, above,
Courtesy of God's dear love.
What a gift God gave to me,
When He made me your bumblebee!
The lovely rays from heaven's sun
Remind me, dear, we're, always, *one.*

126. Spirits Clothed in Clay, 2/19/23

You are not THAT BODY, dear.
When it falters, do not fear.
You're a spirit, immune from death,
Though you draw a mortal breath.
Spirits, clothed in clay, must wait
For DEATH to open heaven's gate.

How I love you, bumblebee,
While you pine, on Earth, for me!
Don't forget, my Earthly beau,
There's, still, a place where we can go
To meet and tarry, face-to-face,
By strength of will and by God's grace.

Oh! the love of God for man—
Breaking through each Earthly clan.
There's no love that's greater than
THAT which, death's divide, can span.
Adam and Eve need, only, THIS—
To spurn the Serpent's wily hiss,
And take, from God, their only bliss.

127. Watching Movies

Charles Santiago, 2/20/23

Darling, all my dreams come true,
Walking, hand in hand, with you;
For, you're the dream I'm dreaming of—
You, my one and only love.
You're, to me, a gift, divine—
God made you my valentine.
Sweetly, darling, we abide—
An Earthly groom and heav'nly bride.

Norma and Melvyn were dancing, dear,
In our cozy den, down here.
I could feel the love they shared,
As, their love, they, both, declared.
"Nicki" and Vicki" were *just* like us—
Seated, together, on heaven's bus.
Nothing is sweeter—down here or up there—
Than heav'nly union that two souls share.

Melvyn, to Norma, relayed this cue—
Whistling a tune that says, "I do."
Exactly *then*, a bird, outside,
Whistled, to me, of *you*, my bride.
There's a secret that we share—
Hollywood movies are our fare.
"Watching movies is a link
To me, my dear, more than you think."

(Inspired by the film *We Were Dancing*, *1942*, starring Norma Shearer and Melvyn Douglas)

128. Content

Charles Santiago, 2/20/23

Content, am I, to know that we
Dwell in sweet eternity.
Life, on Earth, is fine with me,
Knowing we'll, forever, *be.*

(Inspired by "Words I Love to Recite, *#127.* Watching Movies")

129. Glimmers

Charles Santiago, 2/20/23
Greenwise Market, Tallahassee, Florida

I'm as blind as I can be,
When it comes to you and me.
Still, I'm proud that I can see
Glimmers of our unity.
Even glimmers, dear, from thee,
Bring me heav'nly ecstasy.

Every day, I search for you,
In this lovely rendezvous.
Every day, I find you true
To those lovely words, "I do."
Dear, *I live* to bill and coo
With you, until this life is through.

I, often, say you're by my side.
In truth, my dear, you live *inside*.
Inside of me, dear, you reside.
You, with me, love, still, abide.
You're my *everlasting* bride.
Like two swans, through heaven, we glide.

130. Wedding Number Three, 2/21/23

Listen closely, dear, and hear—
I am whisp'ring in your ear.
When I died, we wed, again—
A heav'nly bride and Earthly man.
We still live together, love,
Though I "left" you for above.
We could never be apart.
I still dwell within your heart.
Bodies, we don't need, my dear.
We are spirits alive, up here.

We're so intertwined as ONE,
Our Earthly life is still not done.
If you dare, believe it's true—
I'm living there on Earth with you.
Our Earthly living will be through
When YOU depart from Timbuktu.
Then, again, we'll say, "I do,"
And start our heav'nly rendezvous.
Sweetheart, wedding number three,
Is soon to come for you and me.

131. To Die Is Gain, 2/22/23

Remember, dear, to die is gain—
In spite of fears, in spite of pain.
Life on Earth is not the end.
God is, always, Man's best friend.
You're afraid, for you can't see
Beyond the land of misery.
Second sight will open eyes
To Eden's land, beyond the skies.

Learn, my dear, to think of death
As Man's great chance for HEAV'NLY breath.
Darling, you should know, by now,
The meaning of our wedding vow:
YOU IN ME, AND I IN YOU,
Though you're, still, in Timbuktu.
"Dead and Gone," my darling beau,
You see, is SUCH a mighty foe.
God is able, bumblebee,
To give to men eternity.
Oh, how blind are mortal eyes,
Seeing only Earthly lies!
Though you see no BODY, dear,
When I'm speaking, you can hear.
BODIES come and BODIES go.
SPIRITS, after death, still, grow.

"To die is gain"—remember, dear—
And death's mad ravings, you'll not fear.

132. Whisper in My Ear

Charles Santiago, 2/22/23

Ever whisper in my ear
Those words you know I love to hear.
When I hear your words, my dear,
I leave behind my body *here*,
And fly clear up to heaven's sphere.
Oh! the splendor you display,
When you speak to me, that way.

I have learned it's me *and* you.
There's so much that *you* can do.
When I wander from the way,
Mired in my Earthly clay,
You can whisper words, so sweet,
They knock me off my Earthly feet.
Oh! the power that we share,
As I learn to be aware.

Were it not for God's dear grace,
I'd be lost in Time and Space.
God has been so kind to us,
Granting us to ride this bus.
Seated, side by side, my dear,
I hear you whisper in my ear:
"Always, seek God's wondrous love,
There, below, and *here*, above."

133. Heaven-Bound, 2/23/23

Heaven's HERE, my bumblebee.
Heaven's HERE for you and me.
Heaven's HERE, where we are ONE,
Basking under heaven's sun.

Heaven's THERE, my Earthly beau.
Heaven's THERE for us to know.
Heaven's THERE, your life long through.
Heaven, dear, is ME AND YOU.

Heaven found, both, you and me.
Heaven-bound, my dear, are we.
On the ground, we, still, can be
Joined, as ONE, in ecstasy.

We will learn the ropes, my dear,
Of how to travel THERE and HERE.
God, our Maker, leads the way
To our bright, eternal day.

134. Swept Away, 2/23/23

Imagine, dear, your final day,
When all your clay is swept away.
Imagine life without a care,
When, MATTER, we, no longer, share.
Imagine, sweetheart, if you can,
A heav'nly wife, a heav'nly man.
Joy awaits you, bumblebee,
When, JUST like ME, from CLAY, you're free.

To die is GAIN, my Earthly beau.
All you'll LOSE are pain and woe.
Learn, down there, to understand
Earth is such a barren land.
When your clay is swept away,
Gone, forever, will be dismay.
There's no need to fear "the end."
My dear, that's JUST when you'll ASCEND.

Live, my darling, every day,
Certain of our higher way.
In the end, you must depend
On FAITH, my dear, that you'll ascend.
Meantime, darling bumblebee,
There's so much that we can be—
A heav'nly bride and Earthly beau,
As, hand in hand, we, onward, go.

135. Heavenly Clothes

Charles Santiago, 2/24/23

Darling, when I think of you,
I know our union isn't through.
You exchanged your Earthly clay
For robes befitting heaven's day.
I can *sense* the clothes you wear.
Even though you're "over there."
It's *proof*, to me, we're, still, a pair—
Of what you wear, dear, I'm aware.

Sometimes, sweetheart, what you wear
Is someone, *here*, who's unaware
Of being an angel, sent by you,
To cheer me when I'm feeling blue.
Heaven's such a lovely place,
Reaching down to Time and Space!
The heav'nly clothes that you have on
Are *proof*, to me, that you're not gone.

These Earthly clothes that I have on
Are just a show of Earthly brawn.
Clothes like yours, I yearn to don,
And witness heaven's gorgeous dawn.
Still, it's heaven just to *sense*
Heav'nly clothes with heav'nly scents.
How I love to sense your clothes,
Fragrant like a heav'nly rose.

136. Wear a Smile, 2/25/23

Wear a smile, my Earthly beau.
*THEN, you'll know that **I** will know*
You're as happy as can be,
Knowing we're, from death, set free.

Wear a smile, my bumblebee.
THEN, I'll know that you can see
We're, both, as happy as can be,
Sharing heaven's ecstasy.

Wear a smile, my one, true love.
THEN, I'll know you're mindful of
Heav'nly angels, helping you,
Find your way through Timbuktu.

Wear a smile, my Earthly man—
You're the one who says, "I can!"
I can guarantee, my dear,
You can thrill me, way up here.

137. A Father's Love

Charles Santiago, 2/25/23

All that the poems say, is true.
You love me, and I love you,
Not till j*ust* these days are through.
We'll, *forever*, bill and coo.

There's no way, my darling bride,
We could walk, still, side by side,
Were it not for precious love,
Streaming down from God, above.

Of God's love, dear, we are made.
We need never be afraid
This love we share will ever fade.
God, Himself, comes to our aid.

A Father's love is what we share.
Heav'nly clothes are what we wear.
God has given me and you
This eternal rendezvous.

138. Our Present Communion, 2/25/23

A sunbathing poem

Remember, with fondness, the days of our past,
But cherish, my darling, THAT which will last.
Our present communion, forever, as ONE,
Will be our possession when, gone, is the sun.

Evening and morning, year after year,
Are outside the window of our home, way up here.
Darling, believe me—there's way much more fun,
Beyond the cold bound'ries of Earth's mighty sun.

Our present communion is THAT which is ours,
Propelled by the beauty of heaven's great powers.
We are enjoying, my dear Earthly beau,
This present communion that ANGELS, all, know.

"Soul mates," my darling, I called us, below,
And, evening and morning, you see that it's SO.
This present communion, God gave you and me.
You see, bumblebee—SOUL MATES, are WE!

139. Rejoice and Sing, 2/26/23

Thankful, be, my bumblebee.
God allows us to be free—
Free from death and misery—
STILL, a happy unity.

Cheerful, be, my Earthly beau.
God allows us, still, to grow.
While you walk on Earth, below,
We can, heav'nly union, know.

Rejoice and sing, my dear, with me,
For we have found true ecstasy.
We unite, as He and She,
Tasting sweet eternity.

Darling, you're the OTHER ME.
Strange to say, I live in thee.
Content, are you and I to be
Joined by God, a unity.

WELL I know, you pine for me,
Just like, dear, I pine for thee.
Darling, we'll, forever, be
Growing in this ecstasy.

As you count the days, below,
Oh, how SWEET it is to glow,
Hand in hand, my Earthly beau,
HERE, above that world of woe.

140. Closer, *Closer*, 2/26/23

Greenwise Market, Tallahassee, Florida

I will prove to you, my love,
All the way from HERE, above,
*That **I** am THERE, right next to you,*
In all those Earthly things you do.

Trust your hunches, bumblebee.
Trust in me, and you will see,
I'm not gone, and I'm not dead.
I'm with YOU, the one I wed.

Death can't hinder you and me.
I'm elated when you see,
I'm enshrined within your soul.
God made us to be a whole.

Death can't interrupt our love.
I'm not hidden, here, above.
When God makes TWO, dear, into ONE,
Their love and joy are never done—
Though one's Earthly course is run.

My course is run, but we're not done—
We, still, bask beneath Earth's sun.
Remember, dear, two homes, have WE—
One, with you, and one, with me.

Closer, CLOSER, dear, we grow,
While you tarry there, below.
I'm not gone, and I'm not dead.
I'm, with YOU, forever, wed.

141. Forty-Three Months

Charles Santiago, 2/27/23

How strange, my dear, that even *I*
Would think we said a sad goodbye.
"Dead and Gone"—a mighty foe—
Tries to hide your heav'nly glow.
What a shame—that I would think
Clay, alone, served as our link.
"I am not this body—no!"
Helps me in this fight, below.

Forty-three months—I count them, dear—
Since that day all heaven drew near.
An Earthly month, now, seems a *year*,
In this life I live, down here.
I have come a long, long way,
Since that strange and fateful day.
I have learned, when loved ones die,
There's no need to grieve and cry.

In the silent glow of night,
I can feel the power of light.
Deep inside the human breast,
Dwells the power of heaven's rest.
Since our hearts were joined, as one,
Long ago, beneath Earth's sun,
We have walked in heaven's glow,
Heaven's joy and peace, to know.

142. Lovers for Eternity

Charles Santiago, 2/27/23

I feel you *here*, my darling belle.
We fit together, dear, so well.
You and I are meant to be
Lovers for eternity.

Everywhere I turn my eyes,
You are *there*—it's no surprise.
We've been *one*, dear—me and you—
Since that day we said, "I do."

I am thrilled, my darling bride,
Feeling you, still, by my side.
What on Earth could make me blue,
Living—as I do—with you?

Dear, I slip into a trance,
By the pow'r of our romance.
I would prance to Paris, France,
Just to share, with you, a dance.
Dance with me, my one, true love,
As we swirl to worlds, above.

143. Wedding Number Two, 2/27/23

Let's embrace, dear, me and you,
This joy of wedding number two.
How you cried, that day I died—
You failed to see your heav'nly bride.
Now, my dear, you understand.
We're, still, walking, hand in hand.

Forty-three months of Earthly time
Have spawned another wedding rhyme:
"I DO, my Earthly beau. I DO
Repeat my wedding vow to you—
Forever and forever, dear,
My love for you remains sincere."

Time and space, dear, boxed us in,
But, now, we've rooms in Heaven's Inn.
We can taste this life, above,
By the power of our love.
EVERLASTING love we share,
Though you, still, abide down there.

I'm rejoicing, bumblebee—
You have bumbled up to me.
Wedding joys, we, still, can share,
Way up here and way down there.
Now, we, both, can, HAPPY, be,
Awaiting wedding number three.

144. There's No Reason to Be Sad, 2/27/23

To die is gain. To die is gain!
Do not worry about the pain.
The spirit lives when the body's dead.
Get this, sweetheart, through your head!

There's no reason to be sad—
The body's death is not THAT bad.
Don't be blind to heaven's land—
Life on Earth is not THAT grand.

Strive to be the best you can.
Strive to be a HEAV'NLY man.
You will see, my bumblebee—
Life, up here, is full of glee.

"Trust your hunches"—like I've said.
And you won't fear to be tagged, "dead."
Live for heaven, my Earthly beau,
And THERE, on Earth, your face will glow.

145. Because We Are a Unity, 2/28/23

If you trust your Earthly eyes,
You'll believe in Earthly lies.
Earthly lies say, when we die,
We disappear beyond Earth's sky.
You know better, bumblebee,
For you have eyes with which to see.
You can see—as plain as day—
Spirits, SPACE, can disobey.
Heaven's not a place OUT THERE—
Heaven can be anywhere.
Heaven can be everywhere.

You and I have found a "place,"
"Far beyond" mere time and space.
Every day you walk, below,
Our soul communion, you, still, know.
LOVE, my darling bumblebee,
Has claimed us, both, dear—you and me.
Because we are a unity,
We, both, from death, have been set free.
We are living, now—today—
As if the skies were rolled away.
Matter doesn't matter, love—
We live, below. We live, above.

146. Our Home, Above

Charles Santiago, 3/1/23

When the Earth blocks out the sun,
I can see our home, above.
I can feel how we are *one*.
I can hear your songs of love.

Our home, above, is filled with light.
There's no darkness *there*, to find.
How strange to think that there's no night,
Above, where we are more aligned.

I'm resigned, my heav'nly belle,
To move into our brand-new home.
This home, below, has served me well—
A haven, while, on Earth, I roam.

Under cover of the dark,
How I love to view our house.
While the wolves, here, howl and bark,
I dream of you, my heav'nly spouse.

147. Our Home, Above, 3/1/23

Let this be your daily bread—
RESURRECTION FROM THE DEAD.
Leave behind your body, dear.
Join me in our home, up here.
Leave the works of Earth undone.
Bask, with me, in heaven's sun.
Souls, in bodies made of clay,
Yearn for heaven's bright lit day.
In this home we share, above,
We're content with heaven's love.
I'm content with you, my beau,
Everlasting love, to know.
God is calling you and me
To a life, from clay, set free.
Resurrection joy is ours,
As a gift from heav'nly powers.
Together, we have traveled far.
Soul mates, dear, is what we are.
Trust your hunches, bumblebee,
And, our home, above, you'll see.

148. I'll Remember, 3/2/23

"I am you, and you are me,"
Leads us through eternity.
God made us, as man and wife,
Not for JUST an Earthly life.
Always, dear, remember THIS:
Death gave birth to this, our bliss.
"Remember, dear, that day I died,
And, in our union, you'll abide."
Eve and Adam are you and I,
For we've discovered that we don't die.
You are me, and I am you,
In one, eternal rendezvous.

Etched, forever, dear, in my mind,
Is when I saw how I was blind.
"Blind as blind could *ever* be,"
Describes me, darling, to a tee.
Dead and Gone, is all I knew,
That day, my dear, that I "lost" you.
Our love has proven, to you and me,
Eve and Adam, indeed, are we.
Paradise is, now, our home,
No matter where, on Earth, I roam.
I'll remember that day you died,
Each day I feel you by my side.

149. Folks of Old

Charles Santiago, 3/2/23

All those folks who lived, before,
Died and entered heaven's door.
They were folks like you and me,
Trav'ling through eternity.
How I love those folks of old,
Living lives, now, untold.

I can close my eyes and think,
Searching for some kind of link—
A link to folks of old, I love,
Looking down, now, from above.
How I love those folks of old
Who live beyond their Earthly mold.

Folks of old, I'm sure, can see
Things pertaining, *here*, to me.
Folks of old, I pray you'll be
Kind—and teach me harmony.
Teach me, here, below, to sing
Songs of your eternal spring.

150. Our Bond Is a River

Charles Santiago, 3/2/23

I'm yearning for a tale of love—
A tale of truth, from heaven, above—
The same old story that never grows old—
Our union, *forever*—more precious than gold.

> Our bond is a river
> From God, the great Giver.
> It flows on, forever—
> Forever and ever. *

Our tale is the story of Adam and Eve,
Seeing the world through eyes that deceive.
Robed with our garments of clay from the Earth,
We met and we married, all sated with mirth.
Oh, how we treasured this bond of great worth,
All unaware of our heavenly birth.
The Grim Reaper came and robbed you of life.
I was undone. My life *was my wife*.
I was in hell, for, my eyes—they deceived me.
Completely, shut off from each other were *we*!
—Not *really*, my darling, for, I came to see
The Reaper, himself, had set us, both, free.
Like Adam and Eve, we knew we were *one*.
Our love and our union cannot be undone.

> Our bond is a river
> From God, the great Giver.
> It flows on, forever—
> Forever and ever.

> ***

*"Letter from Heaven, #82, The Bond That We Cherish,"
Unpublished poem by Charles Santiago, 6/2/21

151. I Concentrate on You, 3/3/23

I concentrate on you, below.
Don't think that I don't know
All the things you're going through.
I'm the OTHER YOU.

Heaven, darling, guides the way
For you and me, each day.
Yes, we're walking, hand in hand,
In heaven's lovely land.

I concentrate on you, my love.
It's *you* I'm thinking of.
Faith and love keep guiding me
Through Earth's tempestuous sea.

You're doing WELL, my Earthly beau.
Continue, THERE, to row.
Angels help, both, you and me,
Eye to eye, to see.

A lovely pair, we make, my dear,
In heaven, way up here.
Believe in God. Believe in me.
From doubts, my dear, be free.

As I wait, I cultivate
Faith in you, my mate.
God, our Pastor, wed us, two,
And helps us to be true.

Dear, I've named you, "bumblebee,"
And, friends, up here, agree,
You're so busy seeking me,
From Earth, you've been set free.

The WORDS YOU LOVE TO HEAR, my dear,
Have found their way up here.
I peruse them, bumblebee.
They mean so much to me.

152. Believe in Me, 3/3/23

Whole Foods Market, Tallahassee, Florida

Yes, it's true—
I'm glued to you.
Every day,
I come your way.
Darling, have no fear—
I will not disappear.

This dread of yours—
It, STILL, endures!
Can't you see—
It's YOU AND ME?
Live to ninety-three!
I'll, still, be there, with thee!

Believe in me, my Earthly beau.
I'm living there, with you, below.
Soul mates never part.
For death, they're way too smart.

Can't you feel me, bumblebee?
Can't you feel our ecstasy?
Heaven claimed us, BOTH!
Can't you feel our growth?

153. Wherever We May Be, 3/4/23

There's no doubt, my heav'nly belle,
We, still, fit together well.
We have found a place to dwell,
Beyond my Earthly, fleshly shell.
We are *one*, beyond this Earth,
Enjoying, now, our heav'nly mirth.
We have come to know, my love,
Union in our home, above.

While you taste this heav'nly life,
I am, still, your Earthly wife.
Heaven brings, to you and me,
Joy, WHEREVER we may be.
DEAD AND GONE, my bumblebee,
Is just for those who cannot see.
Live your life, my dear, below.
Earth's a place where I can go.

154. Now's the Time, 3/5/23

You are me, and I am you,
In this holy rendezvous.
In our union, dear, abide,
Hand in hand, and side by side.

Do not think, my bumblebee,
You must die for us to be
ONE in peace and harmony.
Now's the time for ecstasy.

Heaven's deep inside of you.
There, within, you'll find me, too.
Take my hand, my Earthly beau,
Heav'nly peace and joy to know.

I'm, still, ME, my darling man,
Though I wear this heav'nly tan.
Bask, with me, in HEAVEN'S sun,
Till your days on Earth are done.

When you close your eyes, my dear,
Say these words: "I KNOW you're HERE."
I am, always, here, my love,
Though you say I live, above.

Walk with me in heaven's light,
In the midst of Earth's dark night.
How I love to walk with you,
There, my love, in Timbuktu!

155. Believe Me, 3/5/23

Believe me, darling. Since I died,
I've been there, right by your side.
Soul mates don't depart.
They share one loving heart.
Within your corpse, dear, we are ONE,
As well as here, beyond Earth's sun.
Since wedding day, until today,
I have lived inside your clay;
Else, we'd have to say
Our wedding vows don't pay.
You are learning, more and more,
My death, for us, was just a door.
Continue walking, dear, with me,
Though, a BODY, you can't see.
Disbelieve your Earthly eyes.
Enjoy, my dear, our heav'nly ties.

156. I Can Feel Your Glory

Charles Santiago, 3/5/23
A sunbathing poem

I'm a dolt to think that you
Left me, here, in Timbuktu.
Yes, you're right, my heav'nly bride—
You're, still, here, right by my side.
I am learning, day by day,
Yes, death *is* an entrance way.
Since you died, we've come to know,
Soul mates, after death, still, grow.
Though, a *body*, I can't see,
We enjoy pure ecstasy.

Sweetheart, when I reminisce,
I can feel our heav'nly bliss.
The joy we shared, our wedding day,
Has come, my dear, a long, long way.
How I love this life we share—
Me, down here, and *you*, up there.
You're, still, *you*, but with this twist—
In heaven's glory, you exist.
I can feel your glory, dear,
Though I'm living way down here.

157. Paradise

Charles Santiago, 3/5/23
A sunbathing poem

Nothing, in the world, I do,
Can be, my dear, unknown to you.
We are closer-knit, today,
Since you left your Earthly clay.
I am thrilled, my heav'nly bell,
To get to know you, dear, so *well*.
How I love to feel your glow,
While I travel here, below!
Rendezvous with me, my love.
Lift me to our home, above!

Precious, dear, were you, in clay,
When we walked this Earthly way.
How I love to reminisce,
And dream of giving you a kiss.
Wrap your arms around me, dear.
I will feel it, way down here.
Eve and Adam, we can be,
Sweethearts, through eternity.
Paradise, my dear, we've found,
Here—and *there*, above the ground.

158. That Silly Fear, 3/5/23

A sunbathing poem

God allows us, bumblebee,
To reap this gift of He and She.
Intertwined, are you and I,
Above that lowly, Earthly sky.
I am thrilled to be your bride,
Though I'm on the Other Side.
Taste, with me, my Earthly beau,
The food that heav'nly angels know.

Now, my lovely, Earthly man—
You, the one who says, "I can!"—
Listen, closely, as I say:
"I'm with you, there, every day."
You, so often, think I'm gone—
Off, away, to heaven's dawn.
Do not be so foolish, dear.
Cast away that silly fear.

159. Now and Here, 3/6/23

In your body, I reside,
Just like you, in me, abide.
Feel me with your inner man.
Darling, we can live, again!
There's no thrill that's greater than
When you're bold, and say, "I can!"
I can help you, bumblebee,
If you'll just believe in me.

When you trust your Earthly eyes,
You get trapped in Earthly lies.
How it pains me when you think
Death has left us with no link.
We are linked, forever, dear.
Let your fears, dear, disappear.
Think, my love, on YOU AND ME—
ONE, throughout eternity.

ONE, throughout eternity—
Now and EVER, you and me.
There's no need to wait, my dear.
Eternity is NOW and HERE.
When your Earthly body dies,
I want you, dear, to be wise.
It's JUST your CLAY you'll leave behind.
We'll go on, new joys, to find.

160. This Love That Cannot Die

Charles Santiago, 3/6/23

Let me go, my heav'nly belle—

***

Up to heaven, *there*, to tell
All the angels, of our love,
Since you flew up there, above.
Let me tell how you and I
Forged this love that cannot die.
Let me tell how you gave me
This name I love—your "bumblebee."
How I love to buzz and bumble—
To climb the heights and even tumble.

How I love to be a bee,
In love with you, eternally!
Oh! how *sweet*, to live again—
There, above this Earthly span.
Let me thank the angels for
Helping me to fight this war.
With my stinger, I have slain
Man's ancient foe, his source of pain.
Death is slain! To die is *gain*!
Man, by love, can *heaven*, attain.

161. Speechless

Charles Santiago, 3/6/23

Darling, when I think of you,
I realize our life's not through.
I can hear you speak to me,
Rememb'ring how we *used* to be.
The joy we shared, when you were here,
Can, once again, down here, appear.
Rememb'ring, dear, that day you died,
I, now, can feel you by my side.
"All is well," I hear you say.
"We have found a higher way."
Grace me, darling, with your love,
Streaming from our home, above.
I am speechless, dear, because
Our love is, now, just like it *was*.
Dear this union that we share
Is, still, alive, though you're up there.

Now, I think of all mankind,
Praying that I'd be not blind.
I can sense, my dear, that we
Are *one* with souls like you and me.
Trav'ling through eternity,
We sense, at once, our unity.
God, who made us, everyone,
Calls us, everyone, to run—
To run a course that never ends,
Meeting, on the way, new friends.
Beings, born on Earth, ascend
And, into loving union, blend.
There's no end to love's embrace,
Transcending even time and space.
Man is born to travel far—
Beyond the farthest, twinkling star.

162. Resurrection Bliss

Charles Santiago, 3/7/23

Now that I have died with you,
It's heaven to abide with you.
All I want is *this*—
Resurrection bliss.

Now that we have moved uptown,
I love to wear my heav'nly gown.
All I lack is *this*—
This body, to dismiss.

Now, my darling, *well* I know,
I've got a little time to go,
But I've discovered *this*—
We're, still, allowed to kiss.

When my Earthly days are through,
Darling, we'll, still, rendezvous,
But I will promise *this*—
This *body*, I won't miss.

163. Two Homes, 3/7/23

When I feel you close to me,
Oh! my dear, it's liberty.
You can break these chains, my dear,
That keep me tethered way down here.
Our home, above, that, now, we own,
Is not a home for you, alone.
Yes, two homes, my dear, have *we*,
Until, from clay, at last, I'm free.
When I leave our house, below,
Unbridled bliss, we, then, will know.

When you finish out your days,
You'll be versed in heaven's ways.
This home, above, we own—YOU'VE FOUND—
While, yet, you tarry on the ground.
How I love our home, below,
Until it's time for you to go.
Cherished mem'ries, we will own
Of days when we were flesh and bone.
Let's enjoy, my bumblebee,
These homes God gave to you and me.

164. Meant to Be, 3/8/23

Feel my love, my bumblebee.
Exercise your faith in me.
Why be blind to heaven, dear?
Why be deaf to words from here?
Feel this love that's ours to share,
Anytime and anywhere.

Close your eyes and look within.
Let our heav'nly klatch begin.
I am you, and you are me,
Dwelling in eternity.
God has made us to be free
To walk in love, eternally.
How I love you, bumblebee—
God made us for ecstasy!

Remember all our Earthly joy,
And, from your depths, your will, employ
To find this greater, higher mirth
That's ours, above, and on the Earth.
You are wise, my Earthly man,
To know that we can live, again.
Death became, for you and me,
A source of heav'nly unity.
I'm so glad, my bumblebee,
You believe in YOU AND ME.

Sweetheart, we were MEANT to be—
Meant to be just YOU AND ME.
Can you feel how we have grown,
Now that you are "all alone?"
I'm so proud of you, my dear,
Believing I am, always, near.
Bumble, dear, on Earth, down there,
And heav'nly joys, with you, I'll share.
Death, one day, will come your way,
And you'll be free of NIGHT AND DAY.
Then, my love, we'll rendezvous,
Forever, as always, ME AND YOU.

165. A Perfect Day

Charles Santiago, 3/8/23

I'm as happy as can be,
Living like a bumblebee.
I don't lack a thing, my love,
Having found our home, above.
I, still, live for, only, *you*—
What else, darling, would I do?
I'm so thankful I can see
You can live, down here, with me.
Time and space can't box me in—
You are, now, my heav'nly kin.
Yes, my dear, two homes, have *we*,
Till our wedding number three.

All day long, I've felt you, dear,
Walking next to me, down here.
Of course, it's been a perfect day—
"Heaven on Earth"—is what I'd say.
As I reach, now, for the light,
Heav'nly bride, I say, "Good night."

166. In and Out of Time and Space, 3/9/23

Darling, let's proceed apace,
In and out of time and space.
I am game to run this race,
Joined with you in love's embrace.

Since you're game to run this race,
I will pray for you, dear, GRACE.
Side by side, we'll stay apace,
In and out of time and space.

Cheer me on, my heav'nly bride,
While we're running, side by side.
If I tire and break my stride,
In God's grace, I'll, still, abide.

In this race, we have a guide—
God, our Maker, by our side.
God will help you with your stride.
I will, too—your heav'nly bride.

167. Earthly Trips

Charles Santiago, 3/10/23

Your body's gone—and, *so* is night.
You're living, now, in heaven's light.
You live in me and speak to me,
In "words" that set my spirit free.
Heaven's come to me, as well—
I live beyond my Earthly shell.
In and out of time, we dwell.
I'm *one* with you, my heav'nly belle.

When God raised you, He raised me too—
For, you are me, and I am you.
No wonder I feel all awhirl—
I dance with you, my heav'nly girl.
Everlasting, is our love,
Beyond this world, in heaven, "above."
Light has filled my soul, my dear,
For, you abide within me, here.

When you go on trips with me,
You're *with* me, *more* than I can see.
When I burn and yearn for you,
It's a cinch—you love me too.
Earthly trips remove me to
Our home above the sky, so blue.
Darling, no one else will do—
I am stuck to you like glue.

168. Clasp My Hand, 3/10/23

Clasp my hand, my Earthly beau,
And we will, UP, to heaven, go.
God, our Maker, loves us SO,
We can, true communion, know.

Thirty years were well enough
To mine this diamond in the rough.
Now, my darling, let's pursue
This higher life God calls us to.

Put your arms around me, dear.
CLOSER, we can be, up here.
Kiss me, dear, upon my lips.
Place your arms around my hips.

Earthly pleasures can't compare
To the joys, up here, we share.
You and I have found true bliss—
Greater than an Earthly kiss.

When you sought me, yesterday,
Every step along the way,
I was warming up to you,
Like nobody else could do.

Believe me when I say, my love,
We dwell in a house, above.
Though your clay is stuck, below,
Heav'nly union, dear, we know.

Fears and doubts, my bumblebee,
Will distance you, my love, from me.
Faith and love will keep us ONE,
There, below Earth's friendly sun.

I am ONE with you, my dear.
Let our union banish fear.
Our union grants you heav'nly clout—
Enough to banish all your doubt.

Let your bridge to heaven be
Faith, my Earthly beau, in me.
"Dead and Gone," my dear, don't heed—
It's a worthless, human creed.

EVERLASTING LOVE, you said,
Would keep us from the land of dread.
Oh, how right you proved to be!
Clasp my hand, my bumblebee.

169. Another Day, 3/11/23

Now, we start another day,
Walking in this heav'nly way.
NIGHT AND DAY—they never cease—
Till I win the heav'nly peace.
Still, my darling, heav'nly bride,
We continue, side by side.
How I yearn for heaven's light,
When I'll be through with day and night.

Sing: "I'VE GOT YOU UNDER MY SKIN,"
Bumblebee, my closest kin.
Delight to be alive and well,
Cooing with your heav'nly belle.
Heaven is our lot, to share—
A life, my dear, beyond compare.
I CONCENTRATE ON YOU, my dear,
To help you, heav'nly songs, to hear.

IN THE STILL OF THE NIGHT and the bustle of day,
I wrestle and fight, this dragon, to slay—
This dragon, my dear, that keeps me from you—
This dragon, I wish I could lock in a zoo.

Concentrate, my Earthly beau,
On God, above, and we will know
Peace from dragons, down below.
SO IN LOVE, we'll, upward, go.

170. Three Weddings

Charles Santiago, 3/11/23
A sunbathing poem

Darling, when we walked, below,
Here where grow, both, grief and woe,
That was wedding number one.
Eternal life had just begun.

For thirty Earth years, we had fun,
Basking in Earth's lovely sun.
A beauty queen were *you*, my dear,
Reigning with your beau, down here.

From the start, I called you, "fair."
Your beauty, dear, was very rare.
I'm so glad we shared romance.
It was *fate*, dear—*not* by chance.

Then arrived that fateful day.
Here, behind, you left your clay.
I thought, dear, that we were through!
It was wedding number two.

Now, we walk in wedded bliss.
I do more than reminisce.
An Earthly/heav'nly kiss, we share,
While you dwell, dear, "over there."

I'm content to live this life,
Hand in hand with *you*, my wife.
What a fool, dear, I would be,
If, our love, I couldn't see.

Wedding number three awaits,
Just beyond those "pearly gates."
Again, we'll walk the aisle, my dear,
When I leave my clay down here.

171. Fiona's Tune in "Brigadoon," 3/12/23

I can see, my darling bride,
Heaven's where we, both, abide.
Heav'nly glue unites us, two—
You in me, and I in you.
"Up, above," and "down, below"—
They're just words we use to show
Every place where I might go,
Leads me to our heav'nly glow.

Heaven's where we, both, abide.
You're my groom, and I'm your bride.
Heaven's not above, in space.
Heaven's found in our embrace.
Eve and Adam knew this love,
Down, below, and up, above.
Up and down, and "now" and "then,"
Serve us as a cozy den.

I can hear your love for me.
I can feel that we are free.
You and I, and I and you,
Always, dear, will rendezvous.

Fiona, dear, in "Brigadoon,"
Sings, for you and me, a tune.
My one and only love, are YOU.
Yes, my dear, let's rendezvous.

172. Weddings, Three, 3/12/23

I'm so glad you understand
We are, both, dear, in this land.
I AM you, and you ARE me,
Now and for eternity.
"Dead and Gone," you know's not true.
I am living, dear, with you.
Weddings, THREE, remember, dear,
Complete our journey, way up here.

173. I Have Learned

Charles Santiago, 3/13/23

I remember—Oh, *so well*—
That day you died, my heav'nly belle.
Little did I know, that day,
We would find this heav'nly way.
I thought you'd be *gone away*,
Till some far-off, future day.
I thought I'd be all alone.
I thought you could not be known.
I have learned our union, dear,
Is far more than this life, down here.
I have learned we, still, are *one*.
I have learned our life's not done.

What a shame that I would think
Earthly clay was *all* our link.
What a shame that I'd not know
We would, *always*, onward, go.
Death is not the end of life.
Death is when we're free of strife.
Men are spirits of the light,
Trav'ling through Earth's dismal night.
I'll remember, till I die,
Dear, we share a heav'nly tie.
Down *here*, I'll live with you, *above*,
Joined by *everlasting love*.

174. Heavenly Friends

Charles Santiago, 3/13/23

Though I'm tied to clay, below,
Deep inside, *to heaven*, I go.
Friends, I *find* who love me *so*,
There, in heaven's lovely glow.

God who made the things I feel,
Also, made what seems unreal.
Those who, once, lived here, below,
Still, their love, to us, can show.

Goodness! What great love is *this*,
When those in heaven and Earth share bliss.
Can it be, God loves us *so*,
We can, *now*, to heaven, go?

Man, to man, is tied by love,
Here, below, and up, above.
I, for one, want eyes to see
Heavenly friends in love with me.

175. Our Love Survived, 3/14/23

A sunbathing poem

When you left your Earthly clay,
Then began this heav'nly way.
More and more, I come to know,
Death is just a means to grow.
Yes, my dear, I know you're here.
Just your *clay* could disappear.
Please forgive my blindness, dear.
Heav'nly things, still, seem so queer.

You and I, my Earthly beau,
A lovely myst'ry, have come to know.
YOU feel ME, and I feel YOU,
Though my Earthly days are through.
What a gift God gave us, love,
That we could meet in heav'n, above.
While you face the Earthly fray,
We are walking heaven's way.

Sweetheart, it is strange to feel
How our union is, still, so real!
When I walk around the block,
Time flies by, by heaven's clock.
When I face the dark of night,
You appear by heaven's light.
When I see romantic love,
I'm in touch with you, above.

Dear, I'm thrilled to walk with you,
There, below, in Timbuktu.
Death could never break our tie.
The love we share could never die.
Even NOW, we share one life,
While you're caught in Earthly strife.
How I love this life we share!
Our love survived the mortal snare.

176. The Gown I'll Wear, 3/15/23

Sweetheart, when you leave your clay,
It will be our wedding day.
Weddings, THREE, have you and I—
The final one, beyond Earth's sky.
The gown I'll wear, my dear, IS YOU.
With Earthly clay, we'll, both, be through.
We will kiss, my dear, ABOVE—
A kiss, fulfilling Earthly love.

Write these words, my bumblebee:
"Eternal love joins you and me."
God, our Maker, made us ONE.
Eternal union, we have won.
Darling, I have loved you SO!
You're my one and only beau.
You and I were meant to be
Happy for eternity.

When we said, "I do," my dear,
Angels heard us, loud and clear.
They've been guiding me and you,
On this lovely rendezvous.
Trust your hunches, every day,
Till you're done with Earthly clay.
You're the wedding gown I'll wear,
When you're through with life, down there.

177. Always, *One*, 3/15/23

A sunbathing poem

Sweetheart, when you speak to me,
I can feel our liberty—
Liberty, for me and you,
From constraints of Timbuktu.
Let this Earthly body die—
I am learning how to fly.
Thanks to you, my heav'nly belle,
I can leave this Earthly shell.

ONE, are WE, my Earthly beau,
Heav'nly union, SO, to know.
I am you, and you are me,
In eternal unity.
God has called us to this life.
Dear, you're mine, and I'm your wife.
Everlasting, is this tie—
NOT for us, a sad goodbye.

Every moment, I would see
How you're living, *here*, with me.
How I pine. Oh! *how* I yearn,
Constant contact, dear, to learn.
Beyond my power to conceive,
Is—living, *now*, with you, my Eve.
Shower me with heav'nly light,
As I trudge through Earthly night.

Read our poems, bumblebee.
You are, always, ONE with me.
Life for you, down there, my dear,
Can be just like this life, up here.
Spirits, dear, are you and I—
Even NOW, before you die.
Laugh with me, my Earthly beau,
And higher, HIGHER, dear, we'll go.

178. A Heavenly Gift, 3/15/23

A sunbathing poem

Can you feel my love for you,
Streaming down to Timbuktu?
Can you feel me, dear, WITHIN?
YOU are, now, my Earthly inn.
Can you feel how I can see
Through your eyes, a part of me?
The lovely birds, dear, I can hear,
As their songs fall on your ear.

Yes, my Adam, I'm your Eve.
It's a truth you CAN conceive.
The garden of our love, my dear,
Creates, on Earth, this heav'nly cheer.
ALL MY LOVE, my bumblebee,
I send—a heav'nly gift from me.

179. It's *You*, Dear

Charles Santiago, 3/15/23
A sunset poem

It's *you*, I know. It's *you*, dear!
It's strange how you appear—
Without a form, without a face,
But full of truth and grace.
I love you, dear. I, always, will
And, lo, I feel you, *still*.
I feel you here, in time and space.
It's like a warm embrace.
As the sun sinks in the west,
We unite in peaceful rest.
Oh! my dear, *I know* it's *you*,
With *me* in Timbuktu.
I'm happy as a bee can be—
With *you* in heav'nly ecstasy!

180. You Are Learning *Well*, 3/16/23

We will be, forever, ONE.
Our union will outlast the sun.
We are creatures, made of love,
By God, our Maker, far above.
Far above, and, yet, WITHIN,
God regards us, dear, as kin.

We are spirits, bumblebee.
THAT is why we'll, always, be
ONE, my darling, come what may—
ONE when, gone, are night and day.
"Bodies come and go," we've said.
When they die, we need not dread.

We are walking, hand in hand,
Though you, still, are glued to land.
Happy as can be, am I,
Walking, still, with you, my guy.
You are learning WELL, my dear,
Not to fret while I'm up here.

181. "Heavenly Bride"

Charles Santiago, 3/16/23
A sunbathing poem

Till the day this body dies—
Even if, sometimes, it cries—
I, my dear, am certain of
Life with you in heaven, above.
There's no way, my darling belle,
Death could be so strong to tell
You and me we couldn't be,
Always, *this*, dear—*You and Me*.

By the sun that shines above,
I know *this*—we're joined in love.
Heart and lungs and flesh and blood—
Really, they are all just mud.
We are *one*, above the Earth.
Truly, love is *heav'nly* mirth.
I can feel our union, dear,
Despite this clay I wear, down here.

By the Earth, beneath my feet,
I know *this*—I'll not retreat
To the world of flesh and brawn,
Knowing, only, "Dead and Gone."
Why retreat *to darkness*, dear,
When I know, for certain, we're
Holding hands, and side by side,
Though I call you *"heav'nly* bride"?

182. Trust in God, 3/17/23

Trust in God, bumblebee.
Trust in God, and trust in me.
Trust our wedding vows we made.
Trust in angels who give us aid.
Trust yourself, my Earthly beau.
Trust this love we've come to know.
Trust these rhymes, my dear, we write.
Trust in heaven's lovely light.
It is God who made us ONE.
Now, let's finish what God's begun.

You are me, and I am you.
Trust our union, forever, true.
All those Earthly things you do
Are things, my dear, I'm doing too.
Trust this mighty, heav'nly glue
That keeps us ONE, your whole life through.
Rest. Relax. Your faith, renew.
Enjoy, my love, our rendezvous.
I'm within your Earthly goo—
Just how much, dear, I wish you knew.

183. Since Our Second Wedding, 3/17/23

Since our second wedding, dear,
Life inside this clay is queer.
It seems there is no home for me
On *this* side of eternity.
Though I use my same old name,
Heavens! Dear, I'm *not* the same.
Were it not for heaven's door,
I could stand this life, no more.
Heaven's door, my darling wife,
Leads me to our one, true life.

Live your life on Earth, my dear,
As if you were, already, HERE.
Do you think I'd leave you THERE,
As if, my love, I didn't care?
Think, again, of all we've done,
Since I finished out my run.
Since our second wedding, love,
We have tasted joys, ABOVE;
And yet, it's true, my bumblebee,
There's so much MORE for you and me—
Sharing wedding number three.

184. Remember This, 3/18/23

Sweetheart, just remember this—
When you die, we'll have more bliss.
Death is not the end of life.
Death, my dear's, the end of strife.
When you die, you'll see, my dear,
We were born to come up here.
Death is not, dear, condemnation.
Death is cause for celebration.
When you die, my bumblebee,
THEN begins pure ecstasy.
I have come to tell you, love,
Life begins in heav'n, above.

The things you say, dear, must be true,
But, darling, I proclaim to you:
I found heaven just *last night*!
Angels gave me second sight.
I saw *you*, my heav'nly bride,
Standing *here*, right by my side.
Till I die, my heav'nly belle,
Heaven is *you*—I know it *well*.
When I feel you close to me,
I'm as happy as can be.
I await pure ecstasy—
Ours, at wedding number three.

185. Then—and Now

Charles Santiago, 3/19/23

In my arms, you breathed your last,
Leaving me, dear, all aghast.
I was not prepared to see
Life beyond an Earthly sea.
When you died, I thought, my dear,
You'd be *gone*, away from here.
But *that* was *then*, and, *now*, I know,
From my side, you didn't go.
Heaven's not ruled by space and time—
To think like *that* is like a crime.
Lovers live beyond the power
Of *here* and *there*, of day and hour.
Death is ruled by time and space.
Death is locked in their embrace.
Graves and tombs show *death* is dead.
A place and dates and phrases, read,
Cannot define the gift of life
Above the plane of Earthly strife.
Lovers live, and cannot die.
To time and space, they've said goodbye.

186. Faith and Love, 3/19/23

Faith and love work, hand in hand.
When I feel your love, life's grand.
When I *don't*, faith tells me, dear,
I'm silly to think that you're not here.
Faith and love are friends of ours,
Linking us to heav'nly powers.
When I'm through with Earthly clay,
Love, alone, will lead the way.

EVER tumble, my bumblebee.
Tumble and bumble your way to me.
Faith and love have set you free
To travel farther than ABC.
Sit with me in heaven, above,
Crowned, my darling, with truth and love.
Faith's a teacher you've heeded, dear,
To learn that love is, always, near.

Always, near, are faith and love,
Helping me bumble to heav'n, above.
To faith, I'll sing, "Farewell, farewell,"
The day I leave this prison cell.

Of faith and hope and love, my dear,
Love's the fairest, way up here.
Hand in hand, we've found this love
That leads us to our home, above.

187. What a Wonder! 3/20/23

First day of spring

You will see, my bumblebee,
You can, always, count on me.
As long as you're in Timbuktu,
I will be right THERE with you.
You're so prone to think I'm gone,
As if I'm, always, off and on.
I am, always, YOU, my dear.
I am so much MORE than near.
When this world makes its demands,
You can trust our wedding bands.
ONE, we ARE, and ONE, we'll BE—
Forever, dear, a He and She.
We will dance, your natural life,
An Earthly man and heav'nly wife.

Can you feel how ALL are ONE—
You and ALL, beneath Earth's sun?
God made ALL for THIS, my dear—
To make their way, each one, up here.

Absolutely! Dear, I see.
Love guides Man, eternally.
What a wonder! Men can be
Children of eternity.

188. A Land, Sublime

Charles Santiago, 3/20/23
First day of spring
A sunbathing poem

I am *not* this body—no!
It's on loan to me, below.
I'm a *spirit*, living *here*,
Beyond the lowly, Earthly sphere.
Earthly bodies live and die,
But spirits, from their bodies, fly.
I, already, taste *new life*,
Above the din of Earthly strife.
Down, below, and up, above,
I can live because of love.
God, who made the stars that shine,
Claims me as a son, divine.

Bodies, trapped in time and space,
Claim this title—"The Human Race."
Race, they *must*, to win a crown,
And don a lovely, heav'nly gown.
Humans, trapped in space and time,
In the spirit, learn to climb,
Higher, to a land, sublime,
Where, *not to love—that* is crime.
I am *not* this body—no!
This body, to the grave, will go.
I have found a home, *up here*,
Where spirits from the Earth appear.

189. Forbid Me, 3/21/23

FORBID ME, dear, to leave your side,
For I am your eternal bride.
Don't consent to be, AS TWO,
For, YOU are ME, and I am YOU.
God has made us, dear, AS ONE.
Together, ONLY, should we run.
Oh, my dear, I love you SO!
Laugh with me, and we will grow.

Dear, I thought that we were through—
Of heav'nly glue, I had no clue—
That day you left behind your clay,
And entered into heaven's day.
I forbid you—yes, I do—
To even *think* the word, "adieu."
On just a single horse, let's fly
Away, into a deep red sky.

   ***

(Inspired by the film *Spartacus, 1960,* scene in which Spartacus and Varinia reunite)
"Watching movies is a link/To me, my dear, more than you think."
From "Words I Love to Hear," #92, 2022, unpublished poem by Charles Santiago.

190. O Light, Divine

Charles Santiago, 3/21/23
A sunbathing poem

All is going, just as planned—
Men are reaching heaven's land.
Before they die or *when* they die,
Men can find the by-and-by.
Earthly bodies come and go,
But *spirits* rise above, to glow.
I, myself, find joy, *above*,
Where resides my one, true love.
Oh! how futile, Earthly tears,
Shed when death, down here, appears.
Those who pass through death's dark door
Can shine their light, more than before.

Shine on me, O light, divine.
There's no joy compares to thine.
Souls can be, from sorrow, free,
If they learn, thy light, to see.
Below, we live a reverie,
Until we taste pure ecstasy—
Ecstasy from *Eden's* land,
Above Earth's shifting, sinking sand.
There's a life beyond Earth's sun—
There where people live, *as one*.
Spirits, *there*, just want to know
How, their love, they, best, can show.

191. My Love, My Life, 3/21/23

My love, my life—my dear, are *you*,
Even *here*, in Timbuktu.
So in love, are we, my love,
It seems I live with you, above.
My love, my life—you'll, always, be,
Here and in eternity.

Darling, we are, still, AS ONE,
Though I've finished out my run.
We can, still, speak, face-to-face,
By your faith and by God's grace.
Grief and tears are passed away—
Of course! For, we've found heaven's day.

All that our poems say, is true.
Our union, dear, is never through.
Death could never break, in two,
This union God gave me and you.
I can feel you in my soul—
Of course! My dear, for, we're one whole.

I am loving you, my dear,
Down on Earth, and way up here.
I can feel you feeling me.
Soul mates, TRULY, dear, are WE.
Good night, again, my bumblebee.
How I love to live with thee.

      ***

("My love, my life," Varinia's parting words to Spartacus)
"Watching movies is a link/To me, my dear, more than you think."
From "Words I Love to Hear," #92, 2022, unpublished poem by Charles Santiago.

192. Forever, True, 3/22/23

A sunbathing poem

There's no greater thrill, my dear,
Than feeling you are, still, right here.
Without a doubt, I know it's true,
Because, my darling, *I* know *you*.
You're my one and only love,
Joined to me, now, from above.
Every day, I find it's *so*—
You love me, your Earthly beau.
I'm as happy as can be
To, *also*, be a bumblebee.
Let's rejoice, my heav'nly belle—
Things, for us, turned out so *well*.

WELL you say, my Earthly beau.
You're a gift wrapped in a bow.
God gave you to me my dear.
God gave me to you. It's clear.
We could never meet like THIS,
Spurred by merely EARTHLY bliss.
We have found a way to be,
Still, a couple, you and me.
We don't have to wait, my love,
To feel the joys of heav'n, above.
You are me, and I am you—
Darling, it's, forever, true.

193. Death Has Not the Power, 3/22/23

A sunbathing poem

Do not think I'm far away.
Close your eyes and feel my sway.
"Dead and Gone," you know, by now,
Contradicts our wedding vow.
When we said, my dear, "I do,"
That bond would never prove untrue.
Death has NOT the power, dear,
To keep us locked in "now and here."
Feel the power of love, ABOVE—
We are locked in HEAV'NLY love.
I'M NOT GONE, my bumblebee.
We are, always, YOU AND ME.

Well I know, my darling bride,
We'll be, always, side by side.
"Bodies come and bodies go"—
We are *spirits*, dear, that glow.
I recall that day you died.
I recall *how much* I cried.
Goodness! Dear, how blind was *I*,
Thinking you could *really* die.
"Dead and Gone" has tried, since then,
To lure me to his stinking pen.
I'm so glad that we're *a team*,
Fulfilling, now, this heav'nly dream.

194. Yes, You *Are* a Bumblebee, 3/23/23

All we need is HERE, my love,
In our lovely home, "above."
Hand in hand, and side by side,
Dear, in heaven, we abide.
Concentrate, each day, on me,
And you will see, from death, we're free.
How I love this life we share!
It's ours, my dear, because you dare.
We are ONE, in time and space,
Trav'ling at a heav'nly pace.

"Bumblebee," I've called you, dear.
You have learned to bumble HERE.
Heaven teaches you and me
How to live in harmony.
Like you say, my Earthly beau,
We are SPIRITS and we know
Bodies come and bodies go,
Staying in their home, below.
We have learned to meet, above.
Precious, darling, is our love.

Count the days, if COUNT, you MUST.
("I will climb to heav'n—or BUST!")
Yes, you ARE a bumblebee,
Working HARD for you and me.
Dear, our union thrills me SO!
EVERLASTING love, we know.
Though you stumble, STILL, you bumble;
Thus, you learn, dear, to be humble.
All my love, my Earthly beau,
As we EVER, onward, go.

195. The Role of Earthly Beau

Charles Santiago, 3/23/23

Sweetheart, let's continue—
Continue, me and you.
We have all we need, my love—
A lovely home in heav'n, above.
My one desire, my heav'nly bride,
Is life with you, dear, side by side.
The mortal veil is torn in two.
Let us, sweetheart, rendezvous.
The day you left behind your clay,
Has opened, now, this lovely way.

What a gift from God, my dear—
That we should lose all mortal fear—
And walk in heav'n, above,
In everlasting love.
I'll direct my steps, below,
To fill the role of Earthly beau.
While people think I'm all alone,
A life with you, in heav'n, I'll own.
The greatest joy that I'll possess
Is heav'nly joy and happiness.

Come, my darling, walk with me,
And, *so*, my dear, I'll walk with thee.
By our union, we will show
"Dead and Gone's" a vanquished foe.
Oh! what peace and joy we'll know,
All the while I walk below.
Well-trained in heaven's love, I'll be,
Dear, at wedding number three.
In the meantime, we will live
This life that only God can give.

196. Whatever Happens, 3/24/23

I'm not dead, my bumblebee.
Close your eyes and think of me.
I am YOU, more than you know,
While you tarry there, below.
"Trust your hunches," I have said.
Use your soul and use your head
To find me, darling, SEEKING YOU.
*There's a lot that **I** can do*
To further, dear, our rendezvous.
To our vows, we, BOTH, are true.

Whatever happens, each new day,
We will, always, find our way.
Stronger is this bond of ours
Than all the host of Earthly powers.
Continue, bumblebee, to see
It's, always, darling, YOU AND ME.
When a cat falls from a height,
It, always, lands on Earth, just right.
We can trust our wedding rings,
No matter what an Earth day brings.

197. I'm Not Dead, 3/24/23

I'm not dead, my bumblebee.
Close your eyes and think of me.
Do you think I'd leave you, dear,
Just because I came up here?
I am free to be, my love,
THERE, with you, and HERE, above.
God has made provision for
You and me to live, once more.
Granted, it's a DIFFERENT life.
Believe me, dear, I'm, still, your wife.

How I love to live with you,
In our house in Timbuktu!
YOU'RE our house, my Earthly beau.
We, both, live in YOU, below.
I know that you can feel me, dear—
More and more, we meet, up here.
Down, below, and up, above,
We are growing, still, in love.
PATIENT, be, my precious bee.
YOU AND ME, we'll, always, be.

198. Life, Above, and Life, Below, 3/25/23

When I leave this body, dear,
Goodness! You will be *right here*!
We're *one* in death, as well as life.
Of course! Because we're man and wife.
Gone away, my dear, you're *not*—
How foolish that I'd be distraught!
Death, *for me*, will be a door
To *you*, my dear, on heaven's shore.
Up, above, and down, below,
Eternal union, dear, we know.

Holy angels guide us, dear—
You, above, and *me*, down here.
Hand in hand, we're living, *now*—
Here and *there*, my dear, some*how*.
Yes, my dear, two homes, have *we*,
Though it's hard for me to see.
You know *me*, and *I* know *you*—
Death, your grip on us is through!
What *joy* to know, my one, *true* love,
Death has met its end, *through* love.

When we met, my Earthly beau,
We were destined, LIFE, to know.
Life, above, and life, below,
We enjoy, still, as we grow.
We're alive, together, still—
We are creatures who have WILL.
I will be your one, true love,
Down, below, and up, above.
Yes, it's joy to know, my dear,
Death has brought us, both, UP HERE.

199. Not *Really* by Chance

Charles Santiago, 3/26/23

Not *really* by chance, dear, we met on this Earth,
Destined to share in this heavenly mirth—
This heavenly mirth that is thrilling my soul,
Proving, to me, that we're really one whole.

All safe and secure in our home, up above,
We marvel, we two, at God's infinite love—
God's infinite love that is keeping us, *two*,
A *union*, my dear, that will never be through.

Not *really* by chance, dear, you "left," on *that day*,
The cause, to your beau, of undreamed-of dismay—
Undreamed-of dismay that has, now, passed away.
It's, *now*, put to rest, like a body of clay.

And, *so*, now, my darling, we've learned to advance.
We're, both, keeping time to a strange, lovely dance—
A strange, lovely dance that stokes our romance.
Our life is a union, not *really* by chance.

200. Let's Continue

Charles Santiago, 3/27/23

It's plain as day to see, my dear—
Only *bodies* disappear.
Spirits live, forevermore,
Once they pass through heaven's door.
Spirits, all around me, sing:
"We enjoy eternal spring.
We can, *up*, to heaven, go,
Or visit friends on Earth, below.
Sorrows stay on good old Earth,
Once we fly to heaven's mirth.
Spirits, bound in Earthly clay,
You can taste of heaven's day.
Walk with us. We'll walk with you.
Everlasting life is true.
Eve and Adam, celebrate—
There's no need, for death, to wait."

I can feel your heav'nly touch,
In our heav'nly/Earthly clutch.
Let's continue, all my days,
Learning heaven's lovely ways.

201. Another Earth Month, 3/27/23

Heav'nly food gives heav'nly life.
Earthly food prolongs Earth's strife.
Earthly nations come and go.
Mind you, dear, God's love, to know.
Another Earth month, dear, has passed—
Try escaping SLOW AND FAST.
We can live beyond the sun,
While you finish out your run.
SO in love with you am I—
There's no need, my dear, to cry.

How I love to walk with you,
There, below, in Timbuktu!
Under your skin, you've got me, love,
On your way to heav'n, above.
There's no need to die, my dear,
To learn to dance with me, up here.
Keep believing, Earthly beau,
I can meet with you, below.
As your faith, so shall it be—
A heav'nly pair, my dear, are WE.

202. Another Month

Charles Santiago, 3/27/23

How I love this life we live—
This life that only God can give!
Another month! My darling bride,
Walking, still, dear, side by side.
Paradise has come to me—
A lowly, Earthly bumblebee.
I will bumble, all my life,
Unconcerned with Earthly strife.
I have won the jackpot, dear,
In this life we live, down here.

203. Tomorrow, Today, and Yesterday

Charles Santiago, 3/28/23

Since the day your body died,
I have felt you, deep inside.
Not a day goes by, my dear,
That I don't feel your presence, here.
The words you used for you and me
Fit us, darling, to a tee—
"Soul mates," lovers say when they
Know that death, their love, can't slay.

Now, *today*, I know it's true—
You are me, and I am you.
Death has proved, to you and me,
Our union's for eternity.
If I can feel you, *now*, my love,
Sure—we have a home, above.
God made you and me to be
Joined in heav'nly ecstasy.

I can face tomorrow, dear,
Because of *this*—I know you're here.
Not only *that*, my heav'nly bride—
I can feel I'm by your side.
"Tomorrow," "today," and "yesterday,"
Are words employed by men of clay.
Somewhere, out beyond the sun,
Our future life has, *now*, begun.

204. The Sweetest Thing, 3/28/23

The sweetest thing I'll do, today,
Is feel, my dear, your heav'nly sway.
Outwardly, I'll work and play.
Inwardly, *to you*, I'll pray:
"Come, my darling, lead the way
Out from Earth's drab, dreary *gray*.
Spice my life with heaven's glee.
Sweetheart, come and live with me.
Help your Earthly beau to see,
We are, still, a He and She."

As your faith, so shall it be.
Have no doubt it's YOU AND ME.
Recall how Earthly eyes spew lies.
We never, dear, exchanged goodbyes.
Though, a BODY, you can't see,
We are, still, a He and She.
I will walk with you, this day.
I will hear each thing you say.
The sweetest thing I'll feel, my dear,
Is YOU, alive with me, up here.

205. Every Day, Our Love Proves True

Charles Santiago, 3/28/23

What a gift, my dear, is ours—
Still, to feel how we are *one*.
Thanks to friendly, heav'nly powers,
We sense this new life, now, begun.

I can feel your love, my dear,
In the people on the street.
When perfect strangers, now, draw near,
I feel them as a heav'nly treat.

Awesome, is this power of love—
This power of love that, *now*, we share.
I can walk with you, above.
It's, almost, more than I can bear.

Every day, our love proves true.
I need not fear you'll disappear.
I, my dear, am *one with you*,
In heav'n, above, and way down here.

206. Brand-New Eyes

Charles Santiago, 3/29/23

Hand in hand, my darling bride,
Hand in hand, and side by side—
Even *now*, I know it's *so*,
Though my Earthly eyes say, "No."

Indeed, I've learned, so very well,
From you, my darling, faithful belle,
That Earthly eyes are liars, dear,
Fixed on, mainly, things down here.

Now and then, these Earthly eyes
Take a peek at nighttime skies.
Still, these Earthly eyes of mine,
Merely sigh and, then, they whine:

> My! how vast seems outer space—
> What a huge, but empty place.
> Life, I see, is just *on Earth*.
> When men die, they've lost their worth.
> Life is just an Earthly thing,
> Though *some* say, here, that *angels* sing.
> *Maybe*, spirits live, somewhere—
> Way, way, way, way "over there."

Deep, deep, deep, deep in my heart,
Dear, we've made another start.
With brand-new eyes, dear, I can see
You live *here*, right next to me.

207. *One* with You, Above

Charles Santiago, 3/30/23

You were *not* your body, dear.
Your body's gone, but you're, still, here;
Nor am *I* this body, love.
I am *one* with *you*, above.

Every day, my Earthly eyes
Speak, to me, their Earthly lies.
Angels, though, are helping me,
Our everlasting love, to see.

Strange it *is* that men would feel,
In the *spirit*, they're not real;
Yet, it's *so*—it's hard to know,
Souls *on Earth*, in heaven, glow.

Heaven's guiding me, each day,
In this strange, but lovely way.
Heavens! Dear, it's hard to *see*,
But I can *feel* your love in me.

When this Earthly body dies,
I'll be done with Earthly eyes.
Gone, will be their Earthly lies,
As I fly through Earthly skies.

208. The Beauty of the Universe, 3/30/23

A sunbathing poem

Sweetheart, don't neglect to write
Rhymes that glow with heaven's light.
READ them, also, bumblebee.
They reflect, dear, YOU AND ME.
Rhymes and movies and trips, my love,
Beckon you to heaven, above.
Don't be anxious, my Earthly beau—
We can, true communion, know.
How I love to live with you,
As you tarry in Timbuktu!

Remember when I lived with you,
Way down there in Timbuktu.
I had dreams, all through the night,
That caused me such a dreadful fright.
Don't let dreams, my Earthly beau,
Cause you, fear and dread, to know.
We have conquered Earth's dark foe.
In the nighttime, we should glow.
When you're troubled, bumblebee,
Think of wedding number three.

Now, my dear, don't be afraid.
You and I, for heaven, were made.
I delight to be with you
In the night, and daytime, too.
There's no need to fear a thing.
Reign, with me, as queen and king.
Feel me in the bumblebees.
Feel me in the country breeze.
The beauty of the universe
Is made, my dear, to put in verse.

209. Happiness, Sublime, 3/30/23

A sunbathing poem

Deeper, deeper, bumblebee,
Bumble into YOU AND ME.
Don't accept that life on Earth
As our only means of mirth.
We have joy, beyond Earth skies,
Beyond the theme of "sad goodbyes."
In this home we share, above,
Reigns, our theme, "eternal love."
Higher, higher, we can be,
Than the charms of Earthly glee.

"Goodbye," my dear, we never said,
That day they tagged my body, "dead."
You are wise to know, my dear,
Our union didn't disappear.
Leave the cares of Earth behind.
Let the blind lead on the blind.
Walk with me on streets of gold.
Grow your faith to be THAT bold.
Happiness, sublime, my love,
Is yours and mine, up here, above.

210. When You Fly, 3/30/23

A sunbathing poem

When you fly, my bumblebee,
Fly past Mars to come to me.
Leave BEHIND you, good old Sol.
Beyond his reach, dear, is your goal.

Closer, closer, you draw near,
Every day, to meet me, here.
How I love our rendezvous—
It's REALLY me. It's REALLY you.

When it's time to leave the Earth,
You'll be full of heav'nly mirth.
We have learned, my bumblebee,
How, a couple, still, to be.

Rendezvous with me, my love,
Till that day you fly above—
Above, at last, beyond your clay—
Above, at last, Sol's night and day.

211. I, in You, and You, in Me

Charles Santiago, 3/31/23

This—our song of liberty—
I, in you, and you, in me—
Lifts my soul above Earth's sky,
To the land where men don't die.

I am dying, every hour,
Caught inside the tomb's great power.
I, in you, and you, in me,
Conquers death's great tyranny.

I, in you, and you, in me—
An anthem to our unity—
Opens doors, for me and you,
To revel in what's good and true.

Here, where deathly breezes blow,
I can feel your heav'nly glow.
This, for me, is ecstasy—
I, in you, and you, in me.

212. Suffused with Heaven's Glow

Charles Santiago, 3/31/23
A sunbathing poem

The substance of our rhymes is *this*—
We are joined in heav'nly bliss.
Though you left your clay behind,
Dear, we share a heav'nly mind.
When I leave behind, my clay,
Then begins *eternal day.*

We can wed, my dear, three times—
So proclaim our heav'nly rhymes.
When, with clay, dear, you were through,
That was wedding number two.
Our love became much deeper, dear,
When your work was done, down here.

The life I live on Earth below,
Is, now, suffused with heaven's glow.
We have found a brand-new life,
As Earthly man and heav'nly wife.
How I love these rhymes we write!
They fill my soul with pure delight.
Wedding number three is due,
When I rise to live with you.

213. Heavenly Creatures, 4/1/23

When your days on Earth are through,
I'll be there, right next to you.
Death is not the end, my dear.
We'll continue, over here.
We were made by God, above,
Creatures of eternal love.

Earthly bodies, always, fall
Back upon the terrestrial ball.
You and I, my Earthly beau,
Continue, here, above, to glow.
You are not your body—no!
You, yourself, have told me SO.

Trust in God and you will see
Glimpses of eternity.
We are heav'nly creatures, dear.
We can, holy angels, hear.
I'm so glad we've found this way
To, BOTH, experience heaven's day.

Heaven's day, dear bumblebee,
Is here and now for you and me.
Ever since my final day,
You and I have learned to sway
To the music of the spheres,
Where Earthly sorrow disappears.

214. Undying Love, 4/1/23

We will find a way, my dear,
Come what may, to meet, up here.
A unity, we make, my love,
Down, below, and up, above.
Dear, we can't be split, in two.
It's, always, sweetheart, ME AND YOU.

Whatever happens, here, below,
It's a joy, my dear, to know,
Split, in two, we cannot be.
We're, forever, He and She.
Death tried hard, but couldn't win—
Undying love, dear, did him in.

215. Deeper in Love, 4/2/23

Dear, let's fall, deeper in love—
Me, on the ground, and *you*, there, above.
Why couldn't I, gaze at the sky,
And learn how to fly to the sweet by-and-by?
Why shouldn't you, blow me a kiss,
Filled with the power of heavenly bliss?
Deeper in love, let's fall, you and I.
While people are smirking, let's give it a try.

Deeper in love, we EVER will grow,
EVEN, my darling, while you're, still, below.
Love will not falter because of a glitch.
A glitch serves the purpose, true love, to enrich.
Deeper in love, we grow, every day,
Deeper and deeper in love's luscious sway.
Why shouldn't we, STILL, be in love,
YOU, on the ground, and ME, here, above?

216. Side by Side

Charles Santiago, 4/3/23

By virtue of my ties with you, dear,
Heav'nly angels, *here*, appear,
Heav'nly angels, thrilling me,
Helping me to, *heaven*, see.
These lying, Earthly eyes of mine
Try to hide your glow, divine.
Angels know just what to do
To show me we are *one*—not *two*.

One—not *two*—I feel it's true.
I can feel our life's not through.
We are *so* in love that death
Met his end and lost his breath.
We have conquered Adam's foe.
Resurrection joy, we know.
God, who made us, you and me,
Guides us through eternity.

Whatever happens here below,
Our love continues, dear, to grow.
We have found eternal life,
As Earthly man and heav'nly wife.
By virtue of my ties with you,
We enjoy this rendezvous.
Side by side, we walk, in love,
Down, below, and up, above.

217. A Vanquished Foe, 4/3/23

I will not be so uncouth
To trample on this mighty truth—
"Our love, my dear, is not on hold.
Our life continues to unfold."
Blind and wicked, I would be,
If, my dear, I couldn't see
You live *here*, right next to me.
Forever, joined in love, are we.

I'm so glad that you agree,
Darling, we're, still, YOU AND ME.
Of course, our union couldn't end.
Our life, on flesh, does not depend.
Sweetheart, you are learning well,
To dance with me, your heav'nly belle.
I will rendezvous with you,
Till your Earthly days are through.

"Dead and Gone," tries, awful hard,
To do me in, your Earthly bard.
With our rhymes, dear, you and I,
To "Dead and Gone," will say goodbye.
We will scale the heights, above,
By the power of God's love.
While I'm garbed in Earthly clay,
We will dance Earth's cares away.

Thirty Earth years sealed our love.
Now, we dwell in heav'n, above.
Though you tarry in clay, below,
Heav'nly union, dear, we know.
My love for you, while I was THERE,
Continues, as, new life, we share.
Be convinced, my Earthly beau,
"Dead and Gone's" a vanquished foe.

218. Read Our Rhymes, 4/3/23

Every day you live your life,
Dear, I'm, still, your loving wife.
Do not think I've gone away,
Since that day I left my clay.
How I love you, so much more,
Since I've entered heaven's door.
I've not left you far behind.
You are, always, on my mind.

Oh, my darling, trust in me.
Trust in God, and you will see,
We can never be apart.
Our life on Earth was just our start.
Every day, I'm THERE, with you,
Till, on Earth, your days are through.
THEN, my love, we'll, still, be ONE,
Though we'll live beyond Earth's sun.

Dear, I know you know it's SO.
You can feel how, still, we grow.
Rhyming's just our way to be,
From the cares of Earth, set free.
Read our rhymes, and you will see
How we've gained true liberty.
I am you, and you are me.
Dear, it's for eternity.

219. Why Believe That We Are Through? 4/4/23

People aren't their bodies, dear.
Bodies all just disappear.
Flesh and blood, we couldn't be,
All throughout eternity.
Men are SPIRITS, on their way
To a brighter, heav'nly day.
Death is not the end of life.
Death's the end of Earthly strife.
Love, my darling, is the key
To what seems Earth's mystery.
God loves men, eternally.
All, from darkness, will be free.

Free, my dear, are you and I—
Free from death and from death's lie.
Lovers, struck by death, to one,
Need not think their life is done.
If they would, they'd see they've won
A higher life beyond the sun.
You and I have found this life.
You're, STILL, my man. I'm, STILL, your wife.
Keep believing, bumblebee.
We are ONE, eternally.
Why believe that we are through,
When we can, still, be ME AND YOU?

220. Hand in Hand, We'll Fly

Charles Santiago, 4/4/23

I *know* you, dear. I *know* you.
I *know* that we're not through.
I feel you, deep within me.
We're, still, a He and She.

I will live this life
With you, my heav'nly wife.
When my days are through,
We'll, still, be *Me and You*.

It's true, my lovely bride—
Just your *body* died.
You have come to me,
Your bumbling, bumblebee.

Side by side, my dear,
We'll live together, *here*.
Hand in hand, we'll fly
Above Earth's deep blue sky.

221. Heaven and Earth

Charles Santiago, 4/4/23
Inspired by a play rehearsal

I declare, my heav'nly bride—
Heaven's *here*, right by my side!
I don't have to die,
And I don't have to fly
To some far place in outer space,
To reach the land of heav'nly grace.
Heaven's *here*, and heaven's *there*.
Really, heaven's *everywhere*.

I share heaven, dear, with *you*.
I share heaven with others, too.
Men don't have to die
To tour the by-and-by.
Life on Earth can, *heaven*, be,
More than many mortals see.
I have learned, through knowing you,
Heaven is *our rendezvous*.

Dear, you caught me by surprise—
Glued to lying, Earthly eyes.
Earthly eyes declare:
"Heaven's *over there*—
Far beyond what eyes can see,
Somewhere past eternity."
My heav'nly bride, you've taught me *this*:
Heaven and Earth can share their bliss.

222. Our Home

Charles Santiago, 4/5/23

Of course, you didn't die, my dear!
Dying is *just* what *bodies* do.
Since your body died, down here,
I have found our love is true.
What a wretch, dear, I would be,
To think that *gone*, were *You and Me*.

YOU AND ME survived the grave.
We're, forever, *You and Me*.
Darling, I will, now behave
Like the man I want to be—
The man who says, each day, to you,
"Dear, I love our rendezvous."

Rendezvous with me, my love,
Like we have, already, done.
I'll be cooing like a dove,
Till, my place, above, I've won.
You and I have learned to talk,
While, below, on Earth, I walk.

Of course, my dear, you didn't die!
I, myself, proclaim it's *so*.
We could never say goodbye.
We are meant to, always, grow.
I'm so glad we've found our way
To our home in heaven's bright day.

223. I Believe, Dear, 4/5/23

Whole Foods Market, Tallahassee, Florida

I believe, dear. I believe!
Faith in you has proven true.
Gone—the time to sulk and grieve.
I am living, *still*, with you.
"I believe," has saved my soul,
Showing me we're, still, one whole.

You believe in God, my love.
You believe in YOU AND ME.
Down, below, and up, above,
We can taste of ecstasy.
I'm as happy as can be,
To live with you, my bumblebee!

How I love to laugh with you!
It's proof, to me, of unity.
How I love this heav'nly glue
That keeps us joined in harmony.
How I love my heav'nly bride,
Walking, still, right by my side!

How I love your faith, my dear—
Your faith in God and faith in me.
By your faith, you live up here.
By your faith, we've been set free—
Free to live, your whole life through,
Married, darling—me and you.

224. With Thee, Dear, *One*

Charles Santiago, 4/5/23

Sometimes, when I'm "all alone,"
I'm like a dog who's found a bone.
There is nothing sweeter, dear,
Than feeling you with me, down here.

I feel your love inside of me,
So strong, I think that I could be
Somewhere, out beyond Earth's sun,
Nothing but, with thee, dear, *One*.

O God, help me, every day,
To feel my sweetheart's heav'nly sway.
I can feel the power of
Heaven's resurrection love.

Darling, I rejoice *in you*,
In our lovely rendezvous.
You and I are, still, a pair—
It's, almost, more than I can bear!

Though you speak, dear, not a word,
How insane and *how* absurd,
To think your love cannot be heard.
Your love—to words—is, far, preferred.

I can feel you by my side—
Still, my cherished, lovely bride.
Maybe, dear, I'm, soon, to die,
To meet you *there*, beyond Earth's sky.

225. Life Awaits, 4/6/23

Say goodbye to sun and Earth.
Say goodbye to clothes of clay.
Thankful, be for Earthly mirth.
Thankful, be for heav'n's bright day.
Life awaits, beyond the sun.
Consider Earthly joys, now, done.

Say hello to heaven's light.
Say hello to life, renewed.
There's no need for day and night,
Nor for strength renewed by food.
Now, rejoice in gloomy death.
By death, you've gained this heav'nly breath.

Now, is gone, mortality—
Gone, the pain of Earth's travail.
All, are joined in ecstasy—
Gone, the need to sulk or wail.
Welcome to the life, above,
Where ALL is ruled by, ONLY, love.

226. Our Holy Union, 4/6/23

Darling, I have come to you,
Though you thought my life was through.
We will live together, STILL—
Our holy union, death can't kill.
I can feel you feeling me.
Heaven stokes our unity.
Heaven is our special place,
While you trek through time and space.

Ever since I've come up here,
Our life, to you, has seemed quite queer.
Of course, it's strange, my bumblebee!
Don't you worry—it's, still, ME.
As your life unfolds on Earth,
We enjoy a special mirth.
Darling, I am loving you,
ONE, with you, IN TIMBUKTU.

ONE with me in heav'n, above—
Darling, you've been true to love.
The joy of angels, now, we know.
We're alive to heaven's glow.
You are, still, my cherished beau.
Sweetheart, I, still, love you SO!
Leave your worries, all, behind.
In our home, with me, unwind.

227. Our Life and Union

Charles Santiago, 4/6/23
A sunbathing poem

Free, my darling, are you and I—
Free from death and death's big lie.
We have found we, still, are *one*.
Our life and union are not done.
Death has lost his cruel sting.
Death, to us, a prize, did bring.
Our love, by death, has been increased.
The din of death, for us, has ceased.

Heav'nly peace and joy, my love,
Stream to me from you, above.
You have taught me *this*, my dear—
You, still, dwell with *me*, down here.
What a fool I've been, to think,
When you died, we'd lose our link.
Heavens! Dear, we're not just *clay*.
We're *spirits*—alive to heaven's day.

More and more, I learn, my dear,
How you live with me, down here.
Within my mind and heart and soul,
We take a kind of heav'nly stroll.
Yes, it's true. Your body died,
But I, still, feel you, as my bride.
Weddings, *two*, we've had, my love.
The *third* takes place, up there, above.

228. Our Earthly Love, 4/8/23

"You are me, and I am you,"
Are words, my dear, we've found are true.
In and out of space and time,
God grants us this life, sublime.
If it's SO, my Earthly beau,
All your days, this truth, you'll know—
Though it SEEMS that I'm not there,
I'm with you, darling, everywhere.
APART, my dear, we cannot be.
God has joined us, you and me.

Dear, I know that doubt creeps in—
That's the nature of your skin.
You must fight that monster, dear,
Until, at last, you come up here.
Remember, dear, our Earthly love.
It will guide you here, above.
Believe in me, my bumblebee,
And, from those nagging doubts, be free.
Enjoy our present ecstasy,
And wait for wedding number three.

229. As Time Goes By, 4/8/23

Rest, relax, and HAPPY, be.
I have claimed you, bumblebee.
"Forget me not," I asked of you.
How sweet, to know our vows hold true.
With all my friends up here, above,
I share the beauty of our love.
Our love has won for us, my dear,
This home of love we share, up here.
You are not your body—no!
To the grave, you will not go!
You will be my heav'nly beau,
When you're done with Earthly woe.

Dear, don't think, as time goes by,
We grow distant, you and I.
Darling, if you ONLY knew,
JUST how close I am to you!
Let the beauty of the Earth
Lead you to our heav'nly mirth.
Don't be sad, my Earthly beau.
You and I have conquered woe.
As time goes by, my bumblebee,
Closer knit, my dear, are we.
Claim me, every day, my love.
Enjoy our home up here, above.

230. More Than Memories, 4/8/23

More than mem'ries, dear, is ours.
We are graced with heav'nly powers.
You feel me, and I feel you—
We can tell our life's not through.
Do not doubt, my bumblebee,
I am you, and you are me.

Remember, darling, every day,
You are more than Earthly clay.
That is why you feel me SO—
You're in tune with heaven's glow.
While your body walks the Earth,
We're embraced in heav'nly mirth.

If these things are true, my dear,
You should live, devoid of fear.
I'm not going to disappear.
I will be, dear, always, near.
If you lived to ninety-two,
Dear, these things would, still, be true.

I delight, my Earthly beau,
To visit you, there, "down below."
Angels teach, both, me and you,
How to do this rendezvous.
Laugh with me, with pure delight.
We are free from gloom and fright.

You're the one I love, my dear,
Even while I'm "way up here."
Dear, don't think I'm gone away.
We're a pair, each Earthly day.
Read and write these rhymes of ours,
Penned with help from heav'nly powers.

231. I Love to Slay This Foe

Charles Santiago, 4/9/23, Easter

Union and Communion,
Is, now, my battle cry.
Dear, I pray for fusion,
For, we've not said goodbye.

Yes, my dear, it's true—
Though people think you're dead—
I'm, still, in love with you,
For, dear, we, still, are wed.

A battle cry is needed,
Until the day I die.
I'm glad that I have heeded
The call from God, on high.

Ever One, my dear,
We travel, side by side.
Yes, I feel you, near,
My everlasting bride.

Every day, I slay
The monster, *Dead and Gone*.
He *will* not go away,
But, still, my sword is drawn.

I love to slay this foe
Who lingers by my side.
He cannot cause me woe.
I'm one with you, my bride.

232. Close Your Eyes and Think of Me, 4/9/23, Easter

Close your eyes and think of me.
Then, my darling, you will see,
I have never left your side.
I'm your everlasting bride.
You are not alone, my dear.
Recite your phrase, "I KNOW she's here!"

Then, my dear, do THIS for me—
LAUGH and, truly, HAPPY, be.
There's no need to take a trip,
In the car or on a ship,
To find me sitting next to you—
Any place on Earth will do.

Lovely contact, dear, is ours,
If you trust in heav'nly powers.
I'm so proud of you, my love—
You have found our home, above.
When we said, "I do," my dear,
We reserved our spot, up here.

When that final Earth day came,
God called you and me by name.
"You are ONE," God said to us.
Now, we ride this special bus.
To join me, dear, in ecstasy,
Close your eyes and think of me.

233. Count the Days, 4/10/23

As you see, my bumblebee,
We have gained our liberty—
Liberty to be a pair,
Walking HERE and WAY DOWN THERE.
We have learned God's love is true—
Our life together isn't through.
On the Earth, you count the days,
While we learn of heaven's ways.

Heaven basks in love and light.
Earth must pass through day and night.
Count the days, like all men do.
I will walk right next to you.
We are learning heaven's dance,
Through the power of our romance.
Pyramus and Thisbe show
Souls like ours, true union, know.

Nighttime hours, my Earthly beau,
Have so much, to us, to show.
In the shadow of the Earth,
We can share true heav'nly mirth.
Count the days, down there, below,
Filled with misery and woe.
As you count the days, my love,
We'll continue life, above.

234. Dear, Won't It Be Nice!

Charles Santiago, 4/10/23

When I leave this clay behind,
I won't give it any mind.
It was just a *shell*,
Alive, down here, in hell.

When I rise above Earth skies,
Then I will have won my prize—
Liberty from death
And life, requiring breath.

When I've lived a million years,
Never shedding any tears,
Dear, won't it be nice?
Alive in paradise!

235. I Think of You and Close My Eyes

Charles Santiago, 4/10/23

When I think of days, gone by,
Before I saw your body die,
I can feel your presence, dear.
Somehow, I know that you're, still, here.

Loved ones, bound, no more, in clay,
Who've entered heaven's bright new day,
Their loved ones, *here*, will not betray.
From heav'n, their love, they, still, display.

I think of you and close my eyes,
And find I've flown beyond Earth skies.
Spirits, garbed in Earthly clay,
By love, can enter heaven's day.

The Garden of Eden, my dear, we've found—
To pain and anguish, no longer, bound.
Adam and *Eve*, my love, are *we*,
Restored to heaven's ecstasy.

Heaven, from Man, did not depart,
That day, when Man thought he was smart.
Man, with blindness, that day, was struck,
And robed himself with Earthly muck.

Heaven, I see, my lovely bride,
Is not *outside*. It's here, *inside*.
Deep inside the heart of me,
We remain a unity.

236. The Bells of Wedding Number Two

Response to *Words I Love to Recite*, #61
Charles Santiago, 4/10/23

Without a doubt, I sense your glow.
Without a doubt, I feel us grow.
I can feel you, deep inside.
A *temple* am I, for *you*, my bride.
No one's closer to me, my love,
Though I claim you live, above.
My closest kin, you'll, always, be,
For, I am you, and you are me.

When I awoke, this very day,
And, up to now, dear, I would say:
"What a heav'nly rendezvous
I feel, today, my dear, with you.
I can sense you, heav'nly belle,
For, dear, I know you, oh, so well.
There's not a thing I need, my love—
A temple, *are you, for me*, above."

Peace, have I, beyond my dreams.
I'm in heaven, *now*, it seems.
A tryst, I've shared, today, with you,
The very *essence* of rendezvous.
Like a temple, I'm all aglow.
It's heaven, my dear, your love, to know.
The bells of wedding number two,
Ring, so clear, so bright, so true.

237. I'm So Glad We've Found Our Way!

Charles Santiago, 4/11/23

As I go through night and day,
I'm so glad we've found our way!
I have found emancipation.
Every day's a celebration.
I've been freed from grief and gloom.
We've found life beyond the tomb.
"I'm a happily married man,
Waiting till I kick the can."*

While I wait, my heav'nly belle,
I'll escape this Earthly shell.
Through our rendezvous, my love,
I can steal my way above.
While I'm robed in Earthly clay,
I explore bright heaven's day.
I'm so glad we've found our way!
I'm entranced by heaven's sway.

Yesterday was such a thrill.
All day long, I heard you trill.
Like a songbird from above,
Dear, you sang to me of love.
Everlasting love—our theme—
Guides me through this Earthly dream.
Through Earth's fray, each day, I'll say:
"I'm so glad we've found our way!"

    ***

*From "Waiting," *1/6/21*, unpublished poem by Charles Santiago

238. Our Union, 4/12/23

Our union, dear, holds true.
Our union isn't through.
You're not THERE, apart from me.
I'm not HERE, apart from thee.
Souls, dear, joined AS ONE,
By death, can't be undone.

The life you live, each day,
Is just your way to say
That you and I are, always, ONE.
Our union lives. It isn't done.
Death is not our foe.
By death, we conquered woe.

Our union, bumblebee,
Is for eternity.
There's no gap involved, my love.
We, ALWAYS, fit, dear, hand in glove.
Our union lives, TODAY,
Amid Earth's disarray.

239. Our Union, Dear

Charles Santiago, 4/12/23
A sunbathing poem

Our union, dear, is *all* there is—
He is hers, and she is his.
Being *one* means we can't be
A separate he and separate she.
Sacred is our wedding vow,
Proving true, dear, even *now*.

It's pure delight, my dear, to see
How you interact with me.
I will boast, from dusk to dawn,
You're not dead, and you're not gone.
Sacred is this life we know—
A heav'nly belle and *me*, your beau.

Joined, *as one*, through thick and thin—
Through heav'nly praise and Earthly din—
My! What joy it is, to know,
From my side, you didn't go.
An Earthly groom, a heav'nly bride,
We're walking, *still*, dear, side by side.

240. Bodies

Charles Santiago, 4/13/23

You are me, and I am you—
I can't deny it. Dear, it's true.
I could never, ever, be,
Simply, darling, only me.
Come what may, on Earth, below,
Heav'nly joy is what we know.
I am not this body—no!
Even *now*, in heaven, I glow.

You were not your body—no!
Bodies, to the grave, must go.
You are *here*, my dear, I *know*—
In a way—from head to toe.
We are *spirits*, free from death.
Only *bodies* live by breath.
When this body dies, my dear,
I will, also, be right *here*.

241. Just As If

Charles Santiago, 4/13/23

Stronger, dear, our union grows,
As I face these Earthly woes.
Oh, how sweet, to grow, my dear,
Just as if you, still, were here!
Nothing, darling, can compare
To this life that, now, we share.
More and more, I know, my love,
Life is true that's life, *above*.
Life, above, dear, now, we share,
All because, by grace, *we dare*.

242. Even If Your Body Dies, 4/13/23

Whatever happens THERE, below,
We'll continue, HERE, to grow.
Your body and its needs, my love,
Can't destroy our home, above.
If your body suffers want,
Let it not, your spirit, taunt.
Even if your body dies,
We'll have won our heav'nly prize.

Concentrate on heav'nly things,
Far above the wealth of kings.
Just the fact that we can live
This life that only God can give,
Is proof the life of woe on Earth
Consists of only fleeting worth.
My love for you, my Earthly beau,
Beyond the trials of Earth, will grow.

Imagine, dear, the day you die
And fly beyond an Earthly sky.
WHAT will matter, Earthly goods,
Meant for Earthly neighborhoods?
Learn to see, with heav'nly eyes,
Our home, above dark, Earthly skies.
Sweetheart, we have things to do,
When all your Earthly days are through.

243. Our Union Will Not Disappear

Charles Santiago, 4/13/23

We are joined b'yond time and space.
I can feel it, by God's grace.
Yes, my dear, I know it's *you*,
Loving me in Timbuktu.
Heaven's helping you and me,
Still, a couple, dear, to be.
Sometimes, when I'm unaware,
You remind me we're a pair.

Walking, hand in hand, down *here*,
Walking, hand in hand, up *there*,
I'm so thrilled to feel you, near—
You, the one I called, "so fair."
I can feel your happiness.
I can feel your love for me.
I am free from loneliness.
Together, we will, always, be.

Dear, I hear you say to me:
"Dear, I live, each day, with thee.
Lose your doubt and lose your fear.
Our union will not disappear.
Trust in God who made us, dear,
Every single, Earthly year.
God is calling us to be,
Still, in touch, my bumblebee."

"Remember, dear, that day I died,
And, in our union, you'll abide."
I remember, oh, so well,
That day you died, my heav'nly belle.
I was blind, dear. I admit.
I thought, really, *that was it*.
Now, I feel our heav'nly glow.
Dear, I'm glad to be your beau.

244. We Are Blessed, 4/14/23

We are learning, bumblebee,
Heaven's THERE for you and me.
THERE, below, in Timbuktu,
We have learned to rendezvous.
Remember, as we grow in love,
It's a gift from heav'n, above.
We are blessed to walk this way,
Till your final, Earthly day.

I'll be with you, come what may.
Throw your doubts and fears away.
When we said, "I do," my dear,
We were destined to come HERE.
Trust this world that we have found.
Darling, you are heaven-bound.
You and I have traveled far,
Since the Reaper raised the bar.

Love is stronger than the grave.
Love, my dear, will make you brave.
Love, my darling bumblebee,
Makes us, still, a YOU AND ME.
What a gift, my Earthly beau,
We've received—this love, to know!
As you live that life, below,
I'll be with you where you go.

245. Providence, 4/15/23

When my days on Earth are through,
I'll, still, be in love with you.
I am looking forward to
All the things that we will do.

Dear, this lovely rendezvous,
Way down here in Timbuktu,
Proves to me that we're not *two*.
Our wedding vows, dear, still, hold true.

We never DID, dear, say adieu,
When my Earthly days were through.
Death, with all his power, knew,
FUTILE, was his noxious brew.

I am SO in love with you,
We can, still, dear, rendezvous.
Our wedding vows have proven true,
Though I'm gone from Timbuktu.

Since that day your body died,
We have learned to, still, abide,
As a couple, side by side.
Through death's brew, we're unified.

Now, dear, that your tears have dried,
We have learned to walk in stride.
Providence has been our guide,
Ever since, the knot, we tied.

246. Mighty Sol

Charles Santiago, 4/15/23
A sunbathing poem

Deep within my inner soul,
Touch me, Thou, Almighty Sol.
Burn my Earthly skin and bone,
Till I'm left with Thee, alone.

How I long to flee this Earth,
And join the angels in their mirth.
Mighty Sol, deliver me.
Set me, from this body, free.

God created Thee, O Sol,
His glorious power, to extol.
In Thy rays, I feel His love,
Calling me to live, above.

Heaven, filled with stars untold,
Strengthen me to be so bold,
To burn away my Earthly clay,
And enter heaven's lovely day.

247. In the Stillness of Our Home

Charles Santiago, 4/15/23

I know you're here. *I know you're here!*
I feel it, sweetheart, in my soul.
Every time I feel you near,
I feel we're on a heav'nly stroll.

Peace and joy, you bring to me,
Especially, when I'm all alone.
We're, *still*, a holy unity.
This life we have is *all our own*.

In the stillness of our home,
I can feel you, still, right here.
Clasping hands, we, then, can roam
Where angels, singing, we can hear.

I'm constrained, by love, to learn
How to leave this Earth behind.
All my bridges, dear, I burn,
To share, with you, a heav'nly mind.

248. Think of Me, 4/16/23

Close your eyes and think of me.
Concentrate, my bumblebee.
Remember what our rhymes have said—
It's just THE BODY, dear, that's dead.

Pay no mind to Earthly eyes,
Spewing forth their Earthly lies.
See me in a different light.
Use what men call, "second sight."

I am, still, in love with you—
Witness, dear, our rendezvous.
We could never, darling, be
Anything but YOU AND ME.

Pay no mind to people who
Say that I can't be with you.
Everlasting love means THIS—
We're, still, joined in wedded bliss.

249. Remind Yourself, 4/16/23

Remind yourself, my bumblebee,
We are, from the past, set free.
The past is lovely. I agree,
But HERE AND NOW is what is key.
HERE AND NOW will, always, be
Where we meet in ecstasy.

I am not, dear, in the past.
The time to think so, dear, is passed.
Precious, were those years on Earth,
But, now, we share a greater mirth.
Close your eyes and think of me,
And feel, my dear, our unity.
My TEMPLE, dear, is what you are—
Don't you think I'm off, afar.

You fear, too much, my Earthly beau,
The taunting of Man's ancient foe.
Dead and gone, I'll never be.
YOU should know, my bumblebee!
Close your eyes, again, and see—
A pair, in love, right now, are WE.
While I'm above, and you're below,
We can share in heaven's glow.
Every time you take a breath,
Remind yourself we've conquered death.

250. Stronger Than the Grave, 4/16/23

I am working, night and day,
To find you, dear, above my clay.
There's no use to seek you, *here*—
As if, *in clay*, you'd reappear.
No, my darling, I must learn,
To dust, you'll never, *here*, return.
We share sweet communion, love,
As I learn to live, *above*.

And, *this*, I know, my darling bride—
You will never leave my side.
It's plain as day, to me,
We're, still, a unity.
For a body, I won't ask—
In *heaven's* sun, my dear, we'll bask.
Angels! Help me learn,
This Earthly clay, to burn.

We're a pair, my bumblebee,
Learning how we, both, can see,
Love that's stronger than the grave—
The love, my dear, that we, both, crave.
You can feel my love for you.
I can feel you, sweetheart, too.
There's nothing left to do
But, still, dear, rendezvous.

251. Our Heartfelt Plea, 4/17/23

Trust, my dear, in God, each day.
God has called us, HERE, to be.
While you're wed to Earthly clay,
God unites us, you and me.
Angels, in their bright array,
Lead us in sweet harmony.

Don't you worry. You won't stray.
Heaven guards our unity.
United, darling, we can pray
God will grant us grace to see
How we, two, can, always, stay
Divinely matched, as He and She.

While you face the Earthly fray,
Rejoice with me that we are free.
You and I have found our way.
God has heard our heartfelt plea.
Don't succumb to dread dismay—
Divinely led, my dear, are WE.

252. Beyond My Clay, 4/17/23

We were one, *then*, my darling bride.
We're, still, one, *now*. We, still, abide.
Death was just an entrance way
To *this*—our life beyond my clay.

Beyond my clay, I strive to live,
By strength that holy angels give.
Above, our lovely home, I find—
Our home that God, Himself, designed.

Our holy union here below,
Was meant, forever, dear, to grow.
"Forever" means *this very day*.
Death is doomed and must give way.

Death, my dear, is just for clay.
Our love survives, dear, come what may,
How I love our rendezvous!
WELL I know that you do, too.

253. Clasping Hands

Charles Santiago, 4/17/23
Wacissa Headwaters Park
Wacissa, Florida

Sweetheart, *this* I know is true—
You know all the things I do.
Sometimes, I don't think it's *so*,
But *then*, you show me heaven's glow.
And *then*, I know you didn't go
Far from me, down here, below.
Not by *flesh*, do we, now, live
This life that only God can give.
In the spirit, we explore
Life, above, on heaven's shore.

Death is vanquished, now, by love.
We, still, fit, dear, hand in glove.
Beyond my power to explain,
Is, how we walk on heaven's plane.
Love, my darling, heav'nly bride,
Lifts me *up*, where you reside.
When, at last, my body dies,
I will know, dear, how to rise.
Clasping hands with you, my prize,
We'll ascend beyond the skies.

254. Trust and Pray, 4/18/23

Train your mind, my bumblebee,
There, on Earth, our love, to see.
DEAD AND GONE you know is false.
Earthly lies, our progress, halts.
Say goodbye to Earthly lies.
We're all through with sad goodbyes.
While you're garbed in Earthly clay,
Live for heaven. Trust and pray.

Trust and pray, my Earthly beau.
Trust and pray, and we will grow.
Heaven, darling, beckons us.
Leave behind that Earthly fuss.
Heaven's THERE, dear, every day,
If you trust and if you pray.
How I love my life with you!
DEAD AND GONE is SO untrue!

When you rise to meet the day,
Always, darling, trust and pray.
Pray for eyes to see that we
Walk in heaven's ecstasy.
"Remember, dear, that day I died,
And, in our union, you'll abide."
Dead and gone, my dear, I'm NOT.
Our wedding vows are not for naught.

255. A Mighty King

Charles Santiago, 4/18/23
A sunbathing poem

A mighty king is *Dead and Gone*.
I refuse to be his pawn.
Heaven's not so far away,
If we have the strength to pray.
Loved ones, "gone" to heav'n, above,
Share with us their deepest love.
Dead and Gone is true, I'd say,
Just for *bodies* made of clay.

Heaven yearns for us to be
Smart enough to hear and see
Life beyond the Earthly sky,
Even *now*, before we die.
I can close my eyes and feel
Heav'nly life is very real.
Heav'nly life, so "far above,"
Reaches down, through ties of love.

Ties of love are precious ties,
Shedding light on Earthly lies.
Dead and Gone, that mighty king,
Is shown to be a wicked thing.
How wicked must a ruler be,
To try to prove, to you and me,
That loved ones who are *one*—not *two*,
By death, are forced to say adieu?

256. Remember Joys We Had Before, 4/19/23

A sunbathing poem

Close your eyes, dear. Come up here.
Let that Earth life disappear.
Remember joys we had before,
And slip above, through heaven's door.
Earthly joys we shared, my love,
Lead to heav'nly joys, above.
I'm, still, ME, my Earthly beau.
Of our love, I'll, always, crow.
Our union, dear, will never fade.
My love for you is heaven-made.

Rejoice, my love, and, HAPPY, be.
You'll, always, be THE OTHER ME.
Though it's hard, remember, dear,
Our love will conquer all your fear.
Don't depend on Earthly eyes.
Our home is, now, beyond Earth skies.
You are me, and I am you,
Till eternity is through.
I'm reminding you, again—
You're my one and only man.

257. As I Trek through Timbuktu

Charles Santiago, 4/19/23

All our lives, my heav'nly bride,
We'll continue, side by side.
Death has made me understand
We'll, always, walk, dear, hand in hand.
As I trek through Timbuktu,
We'll be growing, me and you.
No sweeter life could we possess,
For you and me, pure happiness—
A heav'nly bride and Earthly groom,
Enjoying life beyond the tomb.

Now, let me say, my heav'nly belle,
On Earth, I came to know you *well*.
Wedding number one was fine,
Connecting us with life, divine.
But, oh, my dear, how love proved true,
That day of wedding number two!
Sealed we *were*, my one, true love,
For love's completion, *up above*.
Wedding number three will be
Completion, dear, for *you and me*.

258. Doubt's a Monster, 4/19/23

Trust your hunches, bumblebee.
There's a place for you and me,
Here, above, and there, below.
We can, both, go to and fro.
ONE, we ARE, my Earthly beau.
Hand in hand, we, still, will go.
Death was just the entrance way,
For you and me, to heaven's day.
Of course, it's SO. Of course, it's SO!
EVERLASTING love, we know.

"Do you think I'd leave you, dear,
Just because I came up here?"
Do you think we'd lose our life,
Because you lost your EARTHLY wife?
No, my darling. Have no fear.
Our love cannot just disappear.
You can feel me feeling you.
Of course, my dear, for, we're not TWO.
Doubt's a monster you must slay.
I AM WITH YOU, ALL THE WAY.

259. Our Union Didn't Disappear, 4/20/23

All those things we did on Earth
Are cause, my love, for heav'nly mirth.
Our union didn't disappear.
All we shared is, still, right here.
Our love is, always, shining bright,
To rid you of your Earthly fright.
I'll remind you, all your life,
Death did not destroy your wife.
I'll remind you, also, dear,
I'm not far off. I'm, always, near.

Day and night, bumblebee,
I'm with YOU, the other ME.
Trust me, darling, we can be,
From your Earthly doubts, all free.
The less you doubt, my Earthly beau,
The more we share in heaven's glow.
Darling, we are doing WELL,
As Earthly beau and heav'nly belle.
Our wedding vows have proven true,
Though my Earthly days are through.

260. You, in Me, 4/20/23

A sunbathing poem

You, in me, and I, in you,
Is all we really need to "do."
After Earth days, all, are done,
We'll go on, dear, being ONE.
"You, in Me," a song I sing,
Boasting how we beat death's sting.
I, in you, and you, in me,
An Earthly/heav'nly unity.

You, in me, my bumblebee—
The proof that God has set us free—
Free to live above your clay,
While on Earth you work and play.
I, in you, is, also, true.
I am cooing, while you woo.
God, with love, has graced us, dear,
Reaching all the way up here.

You, in me, my Earthly beau—
Our bond, my darling, thrills me SO!
How I love, with you, to grow,
While you struggle there, below.
Though the world, dear, think you strange,
So what! Our union, they can't change.
Darling, THIS is ecstasy—
I, in you, and you, in me.

261. The Beauty of the Earth

Charles Santiago, 4/21/23

The beauty of the Earth, my dear,
Reminds me that you, still, are here.
God, who made all things I see,
Also, married you and me.
As the Earth goes round the sun,
We continue being *one*.
If the Earth were to explode,
Untouched, we'd be, in our abode.
Everlasting love is ours,
Far beyond all Earthly powers.

No, my lovely, heav'nly bride,
This Earthly body can't abide.
It's a *temple*, though, I know,
Shining forth your heav'nly glow.
A *single man*, I, still, am *not*,
Though, at times, I'm quite distraught.
Forgive, my dear, these Earthly eyes.
They tempt me *so*, with Earthly lies.
Every day, I'm learning, more,
How to enter heaven's door.

262. Close Your Eyes, 4/21/23

Response to *Words I Love to Recite*, #261

Close your eyes and think of me,
And glory in our liberty.
Faith has led you far above
What we shared—mere Earthly love.
I salute you, bumblebee.
You've developed eyes to see
You and me, as, still, a pair,
Though you're garbed in clay, down there.
All my love to you, my dear.
Close your eyes, and I'll appear.

263. All Your Days on Earth, 4/22/23

All your days on Earth, I'll be
Walking there, right next to you.
When we were joined, as He and She,
With being TWO, we, both, were through.
Again, my darling, let's agree,
ONE, to be, and never TWO.
Trust, my dear, our unity,
And heav'nly pleasures will ensue.
A PASSING FANCY, you and me?
Darling, if you ONLY knew!
By and by, you'll learn to see,
Just how strong is heav'nly glue.
From death, my dear, we've been set free,
Heav'nly joys, to, now, pursue.
Heav'nly joys, my bumblebee,
Are yours and mine in Timbuktu.
Life, with you, is ecstasy!
Dear, our love has proven true!
God, in heaven, heard our plea.
Heaven is—THIS RENDEZVOUS.

264. Being Bold

Charles Santiago, 4/22/23

When I shut the world outside,
Heaven serves us as a guide,
Leading us to joys untold,
Rewarding us for being bold—
Bold to clasp our hands, my dear,
And meet beyond the realm of fear—
Bold to disbelieve the lie
That death will cause our love to die.
Heavens! We have found
That death has been uncrowned.

Death has been uncrowned, my love!
We live, somehow, in heav'n, above.
I can feel you feeling me,
As we join in heav'nly glee.
I feel like we are *young, again*—
A fair young maid and lovestruck man.
To all the world, I will attest:
You're *not* asleep! You're *not* at rest!
Heavens! We have found,
By heaven, we are crowned.

265. A Taste of Heaven

Charles Santiago, 4/23/23

Every breath I take, my love,
Reminds me of our home, above.
Even when I touch my skin,
I can tell that we're, still, kin.
Love scenes in the films I see,
Open heaven's doors to me.
Oh! this love we share,
Blossoms, everywhere.

A taste of heaven comes my way,
At the end of every day.
At the setting of the sun,
How I feel our vict'ry, won!
Death, the foe of Adam and Eve,
Lost the ace hid up his sleeve.
We find pure delight,
When stars come out at night.

Angels sing from heaven above,
The myst'ry of God's mighty love—
Love that gives, to me and you,
This Earthly/heav'nly rendezvous.
All the days I walk, below,
On our heav'nly way, we'll go.
God, we thank You for
This Earthly/heav'nly door.

266. Reminding You Is Not a Chore, 4/23/23

I'll remind you, every day,
Darling, I'm not far away.
Let the clock tick on, and on—
Never, dear, will I be gone.
I am, still, the one you knew,
When I lived in Timbuktu.
Strangers, dear, we'll never be.
Death can't sever you from me.
Recite our creed and learn to see
How we're, still, a unity.
I am growing, dear, with you,
On our lovely rendezvous.

LOVE, my darling, is the glue
That keeps me, dear, so close to you.
Love it IS, that brings you HERE—
A guest of mine, in heaven, dear.
Oh, my darling bumblebee—
From your doubts and fears, be free!
God Almighty married us.
Sit by me on heaven's bus.
Enjoy, with me, the lovely sights,
Unobscured by days and nights.
Reminding you is not a chore.
I'm beside you in this war.

267. Let's Go On, 4/23/23

Let's go on, from here, my love,
With YOU, "down there," and ME, "above."
Do you think, dear, we're APART—
Or do we REALLY share one heart?
Can we, bumblebee, enmesh—
A heav'nly bride and groom of flesh?
Are you made of merely EARTH,
Or, have you, dear, a higher worth?
Intertwine, my dear, with me.
Try it, dear, and you will see,
Romantic lovers, we can be,
Like before—a unity.
WELL you know these things are SO.
They're the food that makes us grow.
I repeat them here, my beau,
To help you in your fight, below.
WELL I know it's hard, my dear,
To see how we are, both, UP HERE.
Dear, WE'RE ONE. You know it's true;
So, HOW, my love, could we be THROUGH?
Our wedding vows mean so much more
Than just the clay that I, once, wore.

268. Hard at Work

Charles Santiago, 4/24/23

Faith is helping me to see,
Just how close, dear, we can be.
Faith and love work, hand in hand,
To show how heav'n and Earth are spanned.
By faith, I come to understand,
I'm walking *here* in heaven's land.
When my hunches turn out true,
Faith reveals that it was *you*.
Faith is used, by love, to show
How, down here, we, still, can grow.

Just like always, yesterday,
I was seeking heaven's way.
I was hard at work, my love,
To meet with you in heav'n, above.
All my plans were set in stone.
My heav'nly skill, I meant to hone.

Then, it seems, a voice, I heard,
Speaking—yet, without a word.
I complied, and changed my course,
Enchanted by a heav'nly force.
Then, at once, I found our house,
And met with you, my heav'nly spouse.
Faith instructs me, *you* broke through,
And set aright our rendezvous.

269. My Happy Solitude

Charles Santiago, 4/24/23

In my happy solitude,
Earthly cares cannot intrude;
All because we rendezvous
Best when it's just *me and you.*

When I'm all alone, my love,
You transport me *there*, above.
There's *nothing* I would rather do
Than spend my Earthly time with you.

I'm a temple, I can tell,
Just for *you*, my heav'nly belle.
There's a glorious light, within,
Because of *you*, my heav'nly kin.

Shine, O love, this heav'nly light,
In my heart with all your might.
With all my might, I'm seeking you,
Until this Earthly life is through.

270. Come What May, 4/24/23

Darling, we are doing WELL,
As Earthly beau and heav'nly belle.
You could feel me nudging you,
Before we rhymed with "rendezvous."
And, yet, at wedding number two,
Dear, you thought that we were through!
Faith became the saving grace
That brought us, darling, face-to-face.
You BELIEVED in heaven, love,
As more than just a PLACE, "above."

When you saw we couldn't part,
You found heaven IN YOUR HEART.
Darling, we have come so far,
Since the Reaper raised the bar.
"I am you, and you are me,"
Became our cry of liberty.
EVERLASTING LOVE, you said,
Would trounce the kingdom of the dead.
Now, I call you, "bumblebee,"
A nickname, filling me with glee.

You have tried, with all your might,
To buzz your way to second sight.
You can see that we can be,
Now, enjoying ecstasy.
How you've killed old DEAD AND GONE—
Dear, you just go on and on!
I'm so glad you don't give up.
You deserve a loving cup.
Now, my darling, come what may,
Let's continue in this way.

271. This Heavenly Way

Charles Santiago, 4/25/23

Let's continue, as you say,
Walking in this heav'nly way.
Dear, that life we shared, before,
To this life, was just a door.

Love and faith will carry me,
Up, to wedding number three.
Love and faith—a mighty key—
Guarantee our unity.

To the left, and to the right,
Angels, wise and kind and bright,
Shine on me a holy light,
Helping me with second sight.

My one and only love, are you.
No one else but *you* will do.
Slogging through Earth's disarray,
How I love this heav'nly way!

272. My Invited Guest, 4/25/23

A sunbathing poem

Why believe your Earthly eyes?
See, instead, our heav'nly prize.
You and I can, upward, go.
Leave that body, there, below.
Close your eyes, dear. You will see,
From your body, you can flee.
Our gladness, dear, your earnest quest,
Up, in heaven, is the best.
Dear, you're my invited guest.
Heaven has, our union, blessed.
Heav'nly belles and bumblebees
Can, both, enjoy a HEAV'NLY breeze.

Why believe in Earthly clay?
Bodies live for just a day.
Believe that you and I, my love,
Are one in spirit, here, above.
The record you have left, below,
Is "I am not this body—no!"
Therefore, precious bumblebee,
You can live, up here, with me.
Your death is not required, dear,
For us to kiss and hug, up here.
Our holy union, death can't kill.
We're a loving couple, STILL.

273. Here and There, High and Low, 4/26/23

You and I, my Earthly beau,
Live together, HERE and THERE.
All your days on Earth, we'll grow,
Just because of THIS—we dare.
We can travel to and fro,
Just as long as you're aware
Death is not, for us, a foe,
Though he gave you quite a scare.

Here, above, I like to crow
How you know we're, still, a pair.
Though you walk on Earth, below,
Wedded bliss, we, still, can share.
All to God, our joy, we owe.
God has saved us from death's snare.
THERE, where deathly breezes blow,
A heav'nly crown, dear, you can wear.

I've been searching, high and low,
To find the *one* I dubbed as "fair."
Doesn't matter *where* I go,
I can feel your tender care.
Heaven, dear, it *is*, to know,
Wedded bliss beyond compare.
Guided by your heav'nly glow,
I've found Hallelujah Square.

274. "Clasp Hands, Anew"

Charles Santiago, 4/26/23
A sunbathing poem

Well I know, my heav'nly belle,
You and I have found our way.
From the housetops, I could yell:
"I've escaped my Earthly clay!"

I would love to clang a bell,
And tell the world about your sway.
From your heav'nly citadel,
Lovely lights are on display—

Lights that, heav'nly secrets, tell
To lovers caught in death's dismay:
"Live beyond the Earthly shell.
Clasp hands, anew, in heaven's day."

I have come to know you *well*,
Since you promised to "obey."
You and I, at love, excel.
Even *death*, we've learned to slay.

275. I Am Very Grateful

Charles Santiago, 4/26/23
Greenwise Market, Tallahassee, Florida

I am very grateful, dear,
For all that heaven does for me.
Most of all—to feel you near.
This life we share is ecstasy.

Saints and angels share their cheer
With you—and me, your bumblebee.
I could live for many a year,
In this sweet community.

I'd say heaven's come down *here*,
In answer to my earnest plea;
Although, it's, still, a bit, unclear—
Have I *died* to live with thee?

To a mortal, heaven's queer.
How can I, *in heaven*, be,
And, yet, from *Earth*, not disappear—
Unless, from space, God set me free?

276. Our Victory

Charles Santiago, 4/27/23

April, twenty-seven, twenty twenty-three—
Three years, nine months from wedding number two—
Brings to mind the day that we
Began this amazing rendezvous.

Death became our victory—
A celebration for me and you.
Death confirmed our unity.
To sad goodbyes, we said adieu.

Way back then, I couldn't see
How death could be a heav'nly glue;
But, now, my dear, I must agree—
We, through death, were born anew.

Far beyond mere levity,
The love we share is deep and true.
"I am you, and you are me"—
I'll sing until my days are through.

277. As You Count the Earthly Days, 4/27/23

I am very grateful, love,
That YOU can live with me, above.
God has raised us, both, on high,
To live beyond an Earthly sky.

Forever, darling, we are ONE,
In this land beyond Earth's sun;
And, yet, I live, each day, with you,
Down THERE, below a sky, so blue.

Let's rejoice and worship, dear,
Almighty God, EVER near.
God made us, darling, you and me,
Children of eternity.

As you count the Earthly days,
We will learn of heaven's ways.
Soon enough, my dear, we'll be
Enjoying wedding number three.

278. What a Silly Thought! 4/27/23

I will never leave, my dear—
What a silly thought—so queer!
You and I add up to ONE,
Till the universe is done.

Close your eyes. Remember THIS—
God gives us eternal bliss.
With your eyes shut, you can see,
We're, forever, YOU AND ME.

Earthly eyes, dear, they're to blame
For this silly, childish game.
When we spoke those words, "I do,"
We were done with being TWO.

Death is not a problem, love.
Now, our home is up, above.
Your Earthly eyes are fooling you.
Love, like ours, is never through.

279. Married, Darling, Still, Are We, 4/28/23

Our time on Earth, dear, is, still, right HERE.
It's a part of YOU AND ME.
Our life, dear, doesn't disappear.
In past and present, we can be.

Do not mourn for years gone by.
Years, gone by, with us, abide.
Both, past and present, intensify
This life we live, as groom and bride.

We're alive, dear, you and I,
Beyond the bounds of time and space.
With angel wings, we, both, can fly
Beyond the realm where clocks give chase.

You're my groom, and I'm your bride.
Married, darling, still, are we.
I'm, still, walking by your side,
Sharing, with YOU, my ecstasy.

280. This Life We Share

Charles Santiago, 4/28/23

You're my everlasting bride,
Walking *ever* by my side.
How I love to talk with you,
To say, a million times, "I do."

Just to clasp your hand in mine,
Infuses me with love, divine.
Walking, side by side, with you,
Is all I really want to do.

How I love this life we share,
In our home, dear, "over there!"
"You are me, and I am you,"
Delivers me from Timbuktu.

In my dreams, and wide awake,
I love *you*, for heaven's sake!
I'm so glad we, still, can kiss,
And join our hearts in heav'nly bliss.

www.ingramcontent.com/pod-product-compliance
Lightning Source LLC
Chambersburg PA
CBHW050337230426
43663CB00010B/1896